CONCERNS AND VALUES IN PHYSICAL EDUCATION

Concerns
and Values
in Physical Education

R. E. MORGAN

Director of Physical Education
in the University of Leeds 1945–1973

LONDON: G. BELL & SONS LTD

Published by
G. Bell and Sons, Ltd.
York House, Portugal Street
London WC2A 2HL

ISBN O 7135 1870 7

Printed in Great Britain by
John Sherratt and Son Ltd., at the St. Ann's Press, Park Road, Altrincham,
Cheshire WA14 5QQ.

Acknowledgements

I wish to express my gratitude to Professor P. T. Geach and Dr. T. C. Potts of the department of philosophy in the University of Leeds and to Miss June Layson and Mr. G. T. Adamson of the department of physical education. All have, on occasions, been kind enough to help me.

I am also deeply indebted to my students on the Leeds M.A. course since its inception in 1969. They have been my most immediate stimulus and their discussion periods have had an influence upon the shaping of my ideas, which can only be acknowledged in this general way.

Mrs. Doreen Walton who typed the manuscript has earned my gratitude, not only for her patience and expertise but for her lively interest in the subject matter.

Finally, I wish to say how much I owe to my wife for her constant encouragement and invaluable help with the text.

R. E. Morgan
Leeds, August 1973

Contents

Foreword

In a theoretical treatise it is well to make the point that physical education is not, in any fundamental sense, a theoretical subject. Like music, art and technology it is, in essence, practical. Its creative power and its social significance lie in its practice. Theory in physical education, like theory in art, music or technology, may, at points, have general relevance but, on the whole, its function is to promote the performance and appreciation of practical work.

1: Definition

Terms not in common usage may be given a meaning by experts: other words can only be defined in accordance with their general currency in the language. Is 'physical education' in common usage? Without question persons connected with education or sport would be familiar with the term and also those in certain branches of medicine. To a parent it is a subject on the school timetable; to a hospital administrator it is an extra qualification some of his physiotherapists have: to the manager of a professional football team it is the new name for P.T. To the head teacher or education officer concerned with values and priorities, it is an idea or set of ideas regarding physical acitivities in schools which not only vary greatly from one group of people to another but tend to change rather radically from one decade to the next.

The first thing to notice is that the term is used in reference to two rather different things: on the one hand it refers to a social need and a piece of professional activity and on the other hand to the science or academic study of this need and this activity. Durkheim[1] pointed out a similar duality with regard to education. 'A science of education is not impossible', he wrote, 'but education itself is not that science'. The same is true to some extent of accountancy and a number of other useful arts. But whereas accountancy as a subject of study consists largely of exercises bearing a very close resemblance to the techniques by which the future accountant will earn his living, both education and physical education as subjects of scientific interest, tend to consist, to a considerable degree, of academic exercises concerned with developmental biology and various aspects of contemporary society which may illuminate but are not part of the professional activity. It is this professional activity which we are attempting to define.

[1]Emile Durkheim, *Moral Education*, Free Press, 1961, p.1.

Some concepts are so firmly embedded into the life and language of mankind that the only appropriate means of establishing their nature is by a process of analysis. Art is an example of this. To define art we must try to discover what the word art means. It would be outrageous to try to indicate what it ought to mean. Physical education is not quite in this position. Although it is nowadays fairly freely used, most people who use it would not pretend to have more than a rough idea of what it means and even experts are known to express uncertainty. It would seem that informed opinion still has the opportunity to mould the meaning of the term. Common usage must be respected, but it can also be clarified and improved.

P. T. Geach[1] has shown that there are two important ways of getting agreement on the use of a term: wide agreement on where it applies and agreement on definitional criteria for its use. Where neither sort of agreement obtains we may get into hopeless cross purposes. But agreement on definitional criteria, or 'conceptual analysis' is not an invariable prerequisite. Some terms have a pretty well agreed application. The term 'physical education', 'P.E.', is surely one such.

The term is sometimes applied without discrimination to any physical activity of a recreative nature. Tennis or ski-ing may be described as physical education. This raises the question of the relationship of physical education and physical recreation which must be looked at later, but to treat the two as self-evidently synonymous (though this is sometimes encouraged by the attitudes of physical educationists themselves) would clearly be wrong.

It is generally accepted that, to rank as physical education, physical activity must 'do you good'. Ideas vary about the nature of the good. Surviving from the days of physical training is the idea of physiological good, and this idea is still strong, but the change of name to physical education has signified an expansion of aim as well as programme. Carlisle[2] indicates the expansion of aim and of programme when he writes: 'Physical education may be taken to label a range of educational activities which are taught, typically, to school children', and he goes on to make a comprehensive list of

---

[1]P. T. Geach, *Plato's Euthyphro*. 'The Monist'. July 1966.
[2]R. Carlisle, *Concept of Physical Education I*, 'Proc. Philosophy of Education Soc.' Vol. III, Jan. 1969.

these arranged in four groups: (a) games, sports, pursuits and pastimes; (b) various forms of dance; (c) gymnastics and (d) fitness training.

Carlisle designates these activities as educational. If he means by this 'provided they are educational' he has surely indicated to most people's satisfaction, where the term physical education applies. The weakness of his statement as it stands is that it could be read as implying that the activities listed are, by nature, educational. It is doubtless possible to demonstrate that these activities have educational potential, and some of them distinct cultural value, but the unworthy purposes to which they are sometimes put, outside and even inside the school, makes it dangerous to assume that too great a part of the virtue lies in the activities themselves. The outward and visible signs must be attended by an inward and spiritual grace if physical education is to be considered as having taken place. The activity and the desired educational effect must become fused into a single happening and to this the term 'physical education' is applied.

This sort of reflection has prompted the attempt to define physical education not as a collection of activities but as a certain *kind* of education—'education through movement' or, less elegantly, 'education through the physical'. This proposal deserves careful consideration because it does attempt to get to the heart of the matter. Many writers have given support to the idea that somatic experience is of particular educational importance. A. N. Whitehead[1] appears to see it as a necessary adjunct to intellectual experience. 'It is a moot point', he writes, 'whether the human hand created the human brain or the brain the hand'. D. H. Lawrence[2] believes that motor experience has a value and a kind of consciousness of its own. He talks of 'acts of primary cognition which are almost entirely non-mental.' The business of the young child in this context is 'not to notice, not to perceive but to ascertain reality'. Ryle[3] seems to stand midway between Whitehead and Lawrence. He would categorise these acts of primary cognition and related overt performances as workings of the mind—though not necessarily of the intellect.

---

[1] A. N. Whitehead, *The Aims of Education*, 2nd edn., 1950, p.78.
[2] D. H. Lawrence, *Phoenix*, 1936, p.641.
[3] Gilbert Ryle, *Concept of Mind*, 1949, Ch.II.

As a definition, 'education through movement' highlights an essential characteristic of physical education but it has two short-comings. Firstly, in return for a certain air of vague universality, it could be restrictive. It could be held to imply that we are educating through motor aspects of experience alone rather than through the total experience of a range of activities, some of them highly organised and socially sophisticated, appealing often to the intellect as well as to the centres of motor control. Lawrence,[1] it is true, would not have us appeal to the intellect. 'You must find teachers full of . . . the zest of fine physical motor intelligence and mentally . . . quiescent. Above all things the idea, like a struggling worm, must not creep into the motor centres. It must be excluded. If we move we must move primarily like a bird in the sky which swings in supreme adjustment to the multiple forces of the winds of heaven and the pull of the earth, mindless, idea-less, a speck of perfect physical animation'. This may be a salutary thought for some of us today. It should put us on our guard against over-intellectualising movement, whether in terms of space, time, weight and flow or traditional mechanics. Movement like art should be appreciated by a process of direct apprehension. But understanding is not inappropriate in art or in movement so long as it facilitates and does not take the place of the direct and primary joy in the activity for its own sake. And surely on occasions we may all feel the need to consider tactics, ethics, good manners, the use of a compass or the relationship of exercise to health. Are we educating through movement? Perhaps we could say we are: but not through movement alone.

The second objection admits of no argument, even if we follow Mason and Ventre[2] in using the term 'psycho-motor activity' rather than 'movement'. Education through the medium of psycho-motor activity includes much that is not thought of as physical education. Much practical work in art and music depends upon the refinement of sensory-motor experience and handicraft is certainly movement education by any standards. Indeed it is often recommended for reasons reminiscent of physical training of the old-fashioned kind.

---

[1]D. H. Lawrence, *op. cit.* p.642.
[2]M. G. Mason & A. G. L. Ventre, *Philos. Aspects of Physical Educ.*, 1965, p.5.

Miss Pontifex,[1] in default of rowing, prescribed carpentering for little Ernest 'to develop his arms and chest without knocking him about as much as the school games did'. Rousseau, in advocating joinery, remarks that it is sufficiently laborious while it promotes diligence, dexterity and taste. There is hardly a teacher of any subject who does not, at some time or other, educate through movement.

We can make progress if we combine parts of the two definitions tried so far and say that physical education is education through a certain given range of physical activities such as those of Carlisle. This indicates what physical educators believe they are doing—educating generally, through thought and feeling as well as through movement—and it makes possible a quite simple and quite exact definition of physical education's field of activity.

The elegance of the definition would be improved, if for our list of activities, we could find some distinguishing mark to serve as a criterion—one which would admit gymnastics and football and dance and would exclude music, art and handicraft. The establishment of such a criterion would open the door to an examination of the manner in which education can be effected through these activities and this should make clear whether they have any common educational significance to bind them together logically into a discipline or whether, failing this, physical education can only be explained as an accident of history which continues its existence because such an arrangement happens to work.

An obvious common factor of the activities in our list is a concern with skill. It has already been pointed out that this does not distinguish our activities from others. Skilled movement enters into very much of what a child does in all aspects of his learning. Enlightened teachers may well see a connexion between physical education activities and these other forms of skilled movement but this does not help us with our definition. Quite the reverse. If we say that physical education comprises those bodily activities which are both skilled and vigorous we get nearer to a tenable position. Yet a boy who is mowing a lawn, or helping to plant trees, shifting properties for a school play or cycling to the library is not generally

---

[1]Samuel Butler, *The Way of All Flesh*, Ch.34.

thought to be engaged in physical education (though, here again, the connexion in real terms is obvious enough). Building a canoe may be considered physical education by the physical education staff but the handicrafts master might dispute this. It is of no great consequence that we cannot in practice put a line round physical education. There is no merit in doing this. But it is important to discover the principles that justify our particular existence.

It has been thought that what distinguishes the activities used in physical education from other physical acitivities is that they are not by purpose instrumental. They do not produce useful objects or works of art or musical sounds nor do they essentially serve a practical purpose, as do handwriting or sawing wood—though they can be put to useful purpose when occasion arises. Their essential purpose and principal justification appears in the satisfaction or benefit derived from the movements themselves. This gets over the big difficulty of including dance and sports while excluding handicrafts, music and the plastic arts. In the latter groups, movement, though of vital importance in the work of creation, is not the justification for the activity nor the criterion by which it is judged. It is instrumental in making an object or a set of sounds. On the other hand, in sport and dance, movement is, or essentially contains, the end and justification of the activity. In some sports and, for that matter, in some dances, the movement may be extended spatially by the use of implements, notably balls. But these have no significance apart from the movement of the players. One can appreciate the sound of music without seeing the movement of the performers; one can appreciate a work of art or craft without seeing the movement of the artist's or the craftsman's hands; but the movement of a cricket ball has no real interest apart from the movement of the cricketers. It is part of a total movement pattern.

The idea that, in physical education, movement provides its own justification has led to an attempt to find a unifying concept in the realm of aesthetics. Carlisle[1] believes that since physical education activities 'offer opportunities for the development . . . of skill and ingenuity for its own sake', these activities 'are best conceived of as aesthetic'. The physical educationist is likely to find this idea attrac-

[1]R. Carlisle, *op. cit.*

tive and stimulating but he may wonder (*a*) whether skill and ingenuity for its own sake is sufficiently dominant in physical education to act as its principal distinguishing mark and (*b*) whether these characteristics are indeed the criterion of aesthetic activity. If they are, then all puzzles, practical jokes and acts of sadism are aesthetic. The word 'aesthetic' surely means more than this.

It is one thing to say that the values of our activities lie in the movements themselves. It is another thing to identify the values. The attempt must be made to identify them. (They may vary from activity to activity, and it must be borne in mind that their values as education may not be exactly the same in character or emphasis as their values in ordinary life.) Aesthetics is concerned with beauty. It is a recognised fact of great importance to us in physical education that our activities are often very beautiful. But even Huizinger,[1] who is on our side in these matters, did not claim this as more than a tendency. It will hardly serve as a raison d'être.

There appear to be two possibilities—one is to give up the search for any distinguishing characteristic in physical education activities. This would make difficult any theoretical justification for their being grouped together and treated as one branch of education but it would not destroy physical education's *de facto* existence. We should have to be satisfied with the knowledge that the grouping of our activities is sanctified by tradition and with the conviction that, with their 'family resemblances', they have values in common.[2] Tradition, in any case, is backed up by the many organisational factors which promote a common approach to the teaching of activities requiring open space and other facilities for free movement.

The requirements for an acceptable definition based upon such pragmatic lines would appear to be threefold. It must contain the idea of education (whatever that may be thought to mean). It must, to be of any use at all, give physical education a field of operation which is its own. And since physical education's principal concerns bring it into such close contact with other branches of education it is essential that this field of operation should be flexibly rather than rigidly defined.

---

[1] J. Huizinger, *Homo Ludens*, 1938, Ch.I.
[2] This view is put by Molly Adams, *Concept of Physical Education II*, 'Proc. Philosophy of Educ. Soc.,' Vol.III, Jan. 1969.

These conditions would appear to be satisfied if physical education is thought of as *a contribution to education effected through a group of physical activities centred upon gymnastics, athletic pursuits and dance*. This definition states the aim, or main concern by which physical education can be distinguished from physical training. An insistence on its right to contribute to general education—rather than to be concerned only with, say, movement education—will have important implications when we later consider its manner of operation. The definition also indicates the field of activity in terms which are specific and yet not restrictive. It seems to be better to stipulate central activities round which others cluster rather than to attempt to define boundaries. The three forms of activity must be flexibly and liberally interpreted. Gymnastics must be held to cover every form of systematised exercise performed with the idea of personal improvement—from Yoga, through remedial gymnastics, circuit training and the callisthenic daily dozen, to the various forms of educational gymnastics and the systems, such as Medau, which border on dance. The whole field of dance would be eligible. Athletic activities must be taken to include all games, sports and accomplishments, including the physically skilled elements in outdoor pursuits.

This definition will serve quite adequately to indicate what physical education is, or sets out to be. It does not go any way towards explaining or justifying physical education's existence. That must be done separately.

The second possibility, which continues the search for a unifying characteristic, is prompted by the form of the definition emerging from the first. The word 'athletic' has been used to characterise all the physical education activities except gymnastics and dance. Can it not be applied to these also?

It will be remembered that two characteristics of physical education activities were identified earlier in the discussion:

(1) vigorous total-body activity which calls for discrimination and skill

(2) enjoyment and satisfaction of various kinds derived from the movement itself.

These are characteristics which might well provide the substance for a dictionary definition of the word 'athletic'. So physical education might quite simply be defined as *education through athletic forms of activity.*

The adoption of athletic quality as a general characteristic not only provides a definition which is more concise and more elegant than that suggested earlier. It carries certain overtones. While it does not limit the scope of physical education to the more vigorous aspects of the forms of movement under consideration, it surely implies that these aspects can never be neglected by physical educationists and that they may, in fact, be accorded a certain priority. Perhaps not many teachers will find difficulty with this idea in the case of gymnastics. More may find difficulty in the case of dance. It may reasonably be contended that the athleticism of dance serves, but does not constitute, its essential quality. If this is accepted, it seems to follow that the athleticism of dance may not be the principal reason why it is taught, even though it is the reason, historically and logically, why it is part of physical education. Dance, in other words, may belong to more than one branch of education; and, in this connexion, particular forms of dance may vary. Surely no dance teacher has anything to lose by this accommodation with physical education, unless, for some reason, he finds the athletic idea objectionable or distracting. Contemporary dancers seem, rather, to find it logical and attractive.

An acceptance of the notion that athletic quality may provide the criterion for and the bond between physical education activities cannot fail to influence the concept of our subject. The interpretation of the athletic idea and its possible connexions with education thus becomes of central importance in physical education theory.

Concerns in Physical Education

Any conceivable definition of physical education must rest for its significance on the conviction that through this form of activity a contribution to education can take place. The possible nature of this contribution is the theme of this book.

Physical education, unlike physical training, the root from which it grew, does not depend upon a preconceived aim except in so far as such an aim can be postulated for education at large. But this is difficult. Education—and with it physical education—is seen as a process which is devious in operation, wide ranging in effect, not easily measurable and permeated through and through with value judgements. It is concerned with the child as he is and as he may become. It must meet his present need for the exercise of his faculties; so it is of immediate import and child-centred. But it must do more than satisfy the child as a child. It must do more than feed his capacity for growth and development. It must direct that growth and development in accordance with what are believed to be the best long-term interests of the child and of society.

As part and parcel of this broad process, physical education is free to operate on a wide front but the nature of its curriculum will lead it to contribute more strongly in some areas than in others. To think thus of special 'areas of concern' is probably more helpful than to think of 'objectives' but in the following discussion the suggested areas of concern will correspond to some extent to the grouping of objectives given in the paper entitled 'The Concept of Physical Education'[1] published by a study group which met under the writer's chairmanship in 1969 and 1970.

Any attempt to identify physical education's concerns or objectives will involve the danger of separating ideas which are interrelated. They form not a list but a network. Gymnastics, athletics and dance are clearly recognisable as different forms of activity. What is true about one is not necessarily true about another and this will be a constant source of difficulty in any attempt to generalise about physical education. But if physical education is our profession we must attempt to see the picture whole, and if we are to avoid the charge of creating a mystique about our profession we must be prepared to say openly what sort of things we think we are doing. We need at this stage a proposition of what appear to be the main concerns in physical education. These can then be discussed in detail, individually, and in their relationship to each other, with the aim of formulating a credible, logical and comprehensive justification for our subject. The justification will come later. The first part of our discussion will be largely analytical and descriptive. We shall be at pains to uncover what is actually thought and felt and done as physical education and to view this against a background of relevant concepts from art, science and everyday experience. The

---

[1]British Journal of Physical Education, Vol.1, No.4, July, 1970.

concept of physical education itself will thus gradually take shape. Some reference to the values commonly held among physical educationists will be made, from time to time, as part of this process but a consideration of ultimate values will be the final stage.

There appear to be five conceptual areas in which physical education is generally recognised as showing a concern. Firstly there is a concern with a discriminating sense of enjoyment and satisfaction derived directly from physical activity in one or other of its various forms. Some people may regard this simply as physical education's recreative function but others may see the possibility of a degree of refinement which confers on it a cultural value. Secondly there is a concern with the teaching and learning of innumerable forms, types, styles and patterns of movement. This points to the need to examine the qualitative criteria by which movement can be assessed, and, in the light of this examination, to consider the extent to which the various manifestations of quality in movement can be accommodated within a dominant concept, such as that of skill.

Overlapping both the previous concerns, but worthy of separate study, is an interest in the manifestations of beauty which may appear in various forms of human movement.

A fourth concern is with the function of physical activity in the promotion of fitness and health. This is our old friend physical training.

Finally there is an undoubted concern among many physical educationists that their subject should take its place among others as a vehicle for forms of education which are not specifically physical in character. It is widely believed that elements of the physical education curriculum may be of particular value in social and moral education and may, when occasion serves, contribute also at a purely intellectual level.

These areas of concern represent different points of view or different motivational frames of mind that may be adopted by the physical educationist when he considers his professional function. When he is working he may be more conscious of one concern than another at a particular time but there is no direct correspondence between these concerns and the formal divisions of the physical education timetable or curriculum.

2: Enjoyment

It has been noted in the last chapter that one fairly general characteristic of the activities that go to make up the physical education programme is that they are not in the ordinary way, productive. There is nothing to show for them when they are done except a feeling of satisfaction and sense of achievement arising out of the activity itself. This feeling of satisfaction may be accompanied by a belief that benefits have been acquired but the feeling is often more direct and powerful than the belief. Pleasurable involvement seems to run as a natural characteristic and a driving force throughout the whole of our work from the movement play of the infant to the physical recreation of the mature adult. Physical educationists will admit that enjoyment does not always constitute an acceptable educational criterion and they may differ among themselves about the particular value they attribute to this factor in their work. Closer study of the forms of enjoyment which are likely to arise from the practice of physical education may enable us to express an opinion. Are they of educational value in the strictest sense or are they just a bonus, a fortunate attribute of our subject material? We are hardly likely to deny that they operate on the credit side. Indeed it may well be that by accepting enjoyment as at least a symptom of vitality in our work and by studying ways in which it can be cultivated we may best learn about its nature and its value.

Forms of Enjoyment
The young child's animal joy in movement, like his other tastes and appetites, stands in need of refinement and reinforcement as he matures in personality. Omitting for the moment the particular pleasures of play, we may enumerate several distinct kinds of satisfaction which are likely to arise from skilled physical action and suggest ways in which these may be cultivated. There are the purely somatic satisfactions sensually derived from vision, touch, balance

and varying muscular tension. These can be augmented by an extension of the skill range. Learning to climb, to swim or to ride a bicycle will bring new sensations of pleasure. Along with this the child can be encouraged to use his mastery of skill as approach to new inter-personal experience of many kinds. Skilled physical activity, whether competitive, co-operative or just practised in company, has the power to arouse interest and feeling among participants. It should be the concern of teachers to direct this interest and feeling towards ends which are socially acceptable and personally rewarding, towards community of interest and fellow feeling even among rival protagonists. It is undoubtedly in the nature of many of the activities in the physical education programme that they may find expression in laughter and a sense of fun. This is a self-evident value. Closely allied to the fun may be an awareness of beauty—either of the movement form itself or of the movement in its setting. Often a movement which is unremarkable in itself—like walking across a cricket field or rowing across a lake—may take significance from its setting. It may even give significance to its setting. Appreciation for the observer embraces both. The mover himself is rarely conscious of his own movements in a visual way but often in everyday life, and very often in athletics and dance, he is caught up in a group movement in which he is both participant and observer and here his double enjoyment may well be more vivid than that of a spectator. One source of delight arising from movement is certainly the opportunity it gives to explore an environment. The unadventurous or handicapped child may particularly benefit from the help of physical education in extending and enriching this exploration.

These three elements, aesthetic, somatic and inter-personal, may combine to produce the state of psychic satisfaction associated with release of tensions which is so often sought and found in physical activity. A memorable passage from *The Plague* by Albert Camus[1] expresses this well:

> " 'Do you know,' he said, 'what we now should do for friendship's sake?'
> 'Anything you like, Tarrou.'

---

[1]Albert Camus, *The Plague*, transl. Stuart Gilbert, 1948, Part 4, Ch.6.

'Go for a swim. It's one of these harmless pleasures that even a saint-to-be can indulge in. . . . Really it's too damn silly living only in and for the plague.' . . . Rieux dived in first. After the first shock of cold had passed and he came back to the surface the water seemed tepid. When he had taken a few strokes he found that the sea was warm that night with the warmth of autumn seas that borrow from the shore the accumulated heat of the long days of summer. The movement of his feet left a foaming wake as he swam steadily ahead, and the water slipped along his arms to close in tightly on his legs. A loud splash told him that Tarrou had dived. Rieux lay on his back and stayed motionless, gazing up at the dome of sky lit by the stars and moon. He drew a deep breath. Then he heard a sound of beaten water, louder and louder, amazingly clear in the hollow silence of the night. Tarrou was coming up with him. He now could hear his breathing.

Rieux turned and swam level with his friend, timing his stroke to his. But Tarrou was the stronger swimmer and Rieux had to put on speed to keep up with him. For some minutes they swam side by side, with the same zest, in the same rhythm, isolated from the world, at last free of the town and of the plague. Rieux was the first to stop and they swam back slowly, except at one point, where unexpectedly they found themselves caught in an ice-cold current. Their energy whipped up by this trap the sea had sprung on them, both struck out more vigorously.

They dressed and started back. Neither had said a word, but they were conscious of being perfectly at one."

Effects of Teaching

The charge is sometimes made that organisation and teaching may restrict or extinguish enjoyment of this kind. Certainly there is a danger, and it may be useful at this point to draw attention to those faults in presentation which can have an adverse effect upon the child's attitude towards physical activity as represented in the physical education programme. The first is undoubtedly the insensitive teaching which takes no account of the enthusiasms of the child, which acts as a brake on spontaneity and does not even notice when the child is getting bored. Secondly there may be too great an insistence on standards of performance with less able children, particularly in activities where failure can be painful or humiliating. Thirdly there may be an unintelligent introduction to rigorous activities of a training nature such as circuit training or cross-country running. Training can be enjoyable enough but it is of little value unless the reasons for it are understood and accepted. They are only likely to be understood and accepted when enthusiasm already exists. Fourthly there may be wrong handling of the element of competition. Competition is an essential part of a whole range of games and contests which boys and girls have traditionally enjoyed, and, rightly handled, the competitive element may raise the level of interest to a point of high excitement which is still completely enjoyable. But it can have the effect of bringing individual deficiencies into prominence, it can cloak rough and insensitive behaviour and it can be used to confer on games and athletics a status which appears to many people as out of all proportion to their true value as play.

The converse of these errors is the deliberate cultivation of an atmosphere in physical education where skilled movement is recognised by teachers and pupils not solely, or even primarily, as a type of performance governed by external standards which some may attain and others may not, but as a human birthright like sight, hearing and natural affection. Every child has a right to exercise it: every child has the means to attain it. This includes even the severely handicapped; in fact it applies to them with particular force. For the performer the value and significance of skill cannot be quantified. Under favourable conditions the poor performer may obtain as much personal pleasure and satisfaction as the good performer. Educationally the important question is not whether a particular child is good at games or good at gymnastics or good at dance. It is whether games, gymnastics and dance are being presented to him in a form and manner which will bring him most benefit. Enjoyment is surely part of the benefit.

It is this point which justifies the differentiation of enjoyment and skill as concerns in physical education. They are clearly related to each other. An access of skill is one of the most powerful sources of enjoyment. But there are times when the degree of skill just does not matter. In the incident quoted above it does not matter that Tarrou is a better swimmer than Rieux. What matters is that they both have enough skill to enjoy swimming. To be able to do something well enough to enjoy it, to use it creatively and 'for friendship's sake' is a worthwhile aim and is not without value as a challenge to the learner; but it is a challenge of a different order from that presented by the desire to excel. Physical education must accommodate itself to both forms of challenge. For some persons there is no lasting appeal without the opportunity to test performance and improvement against external standards. Their attitude is neither more nor less worthy than that of people who take a less competitive interest in skilled activity. The point that concerns us here is how the teacher of physical education can best hope to ensure that the acceptance of the idea of competitive standards does not overshadow the equally valid and, perhaps, educationally more important idea of competence for its own sake. The need for this reconciliation between different attitudes and inclinations is present throughout the range of physical education activities. Even in so-called non-competitive activities such as rock climbing or dance, there are some who will react unfavourably if forced to take things too seriously. But it is in the realm of competitive play that the differences of attitude are most acute.

Play, Work and Practice

The idea of play is very strongly associated with physical education and this sometimes causes us misgivings about the educational status of our subject. R. F. Dearden[1] tells us: 'Play is non-serious . . . it has no ethical value. . . . What we play at is intrinsically unimportant'. There is clearly a point up to which this is true—sufficient to make it worthwhile for us to review the qualities by which play can be recognised (that is distinguished from non-play) and by which its relationship to the idea of work can be established in order that we may test the strength and significance of the link between the idea of play and our subject.

The relationship of the concepts of play and work can be clarified to some extent on the grounds of effort, pleasure and motive. Work is effortful activity performed primarily for the attainment of some

---

[1] R. F. Dearden, *Philosophy of Primary Education*, 1968, Ch.5.

external objective. Work may or may not be voluntarily undertaken and it may be pleasant or unpleasant but among free men the idea of moral compulsion and of the dignity of work is strong. We feel we ought to work; we demand the right to work. Play is voluntary and pleasant. It may or may not be effortful and though an external objective is not incompatible with play it is not part of the essential idea which demands a motive internal to the activity. A professional may continue to be a player in the truest sense of the word: indeed a good professional is usually enough of an artist to enter into the spirit of the game, and, when actually playing, to play for the excitement or the interest or the fun to be found in the activity. He may, of course, lose this interest and then, like the unwilling participant in compulsory games at school, he is a player in name only. But, both for the schoolboy and the professional, true play may include work. We often say that a player is working hard; his activity is effortful and he has a clear-cut objective in mind. That is not to confuse the concepts of work and play. The distinguishing mark of play is the acceptance of a form of 'make-believe' by the participants, one or many. The kitten and its mother both accept the make-believe nature of their mutual hostility. A child who is pretending to keep house is playing; if he is helping his mother in the house he is not playing, though he may enjoy it equally. The freely accepted rules in more sophisticated games provide the structure of pretence which liberates the participants from certain of the more general laws, natural, political or economic, which govern the matter-of-fact, non-play activities of normal life. But they do not liberate them from all such general laws. The artificiality is a matter of degree. We could imagine a game where—with the aid of hydrogen-filled suits—the law of gravity was cancelled, and, in certain frivolous situations, people may indeed play a game in which some of the normal moral laws are ignored, to the extent that even cheating is allowed so long as the result is amusing. But most games are much nearer normal life than this. Certain rules or conventions are adopted, which, to a lesser or a greater extent, provide an element of divorce from real life. Apart from these conventions the rules of normal life apply. Dearden[1] concedes that: 'In culpable cases, of

---

[1] R. F. Dearden, *op. cit.*

course, the play is culpable because really the activity is a serious matter'. One is inclined to think that there can be an element of seriousness in other cases too. In some forms of athletics, say a track race or a boxing match, the element of make-believe is so slim and the relevance of normal physical and moral laws is so strong that one doubts whether these activities are, in fact, in game form. But there are many true games which are near enough to the style of normal life for performance in them to be taken as having general significance. To know that a person is an expert chess player or that he is always scrupulously fair and unruffled at football tells you something about him as a person. He does not become a different person when he starts or stops playing. The difference in his conduct will depend not upon the fact of his playing but upon the attitudes he believes the particular form of play demands from him—serious application and a strict attention to behavioural standards or a light-hearted renunciation of responsibility. The mistake is to think that play is a uniform phenomenon. Ring-a-roses, Cops and Robbers and Monopoly may indeed have no intrinsic importance or ethical value, but these are only juveniles or, at best, poor relations in the great family of games.

One or two ideas emerge out of this which appear to be of significance in considering the enjoyment factor in physical education. Practice is simpler than play. Play, as an artificial activity, seems to demand a certain level of sophistication in the participants. At first the young child and the young animal are too immature to play at all. The exploratory movements of the kitten a few weeks old have nothing of play about them. These practice movements are, perhaps, not consciously objective enough to be called work, but the degree of effort, the obvious compulsion to persist in face of failures and the survival value of the actions involved make them more akin to work than play. The same is true of the early practice movements of the young child and though he will be capable of understanding certain simple forms of play before he comes to school his early contact with physical education will probably not be through play but through the serious investigation of movement problems and the serious acquisition of skills. He will be fascinated by this. There is certainly no need to introduce play activities for the sake of enjoyment.

Though in the very early years of school physical education the idea of practice is stronger than the idea of play, play will find its way into the programme. Perhaps the earliest forms of play in the physical education context will be contrived additions to the practice movements such as clapping between catches of a bouncing ball. Eventually play will take the form of organised competitive games. In this country most children are introduced to these games and are given good facilities and every encouragement to play. Not all children develop a liking for games. Some positively come to dislike them but the fact must be recognised that among older adolescents and young adults who continue voluntary participation in physical education activities the majority do so in the form of competitive games of one kind or another. Certainly the traditional physical education programme for older boys and girls in this country or anywhere in the world consists to a large extent of games.

As we have seen, enjoyment of skilled physical action may exist in various forms independently of play. Serious practice and even hard work may be enjoyable. We have also seen that a play element can introduce itself into an activity without destroying the seriousness or the relevance of that activity, whatever this seriousness or relevance may be, but the justification of introducing a play element can only be to increase the enjoyment in some way or another. Young boys climbing a tree might increase their enjoyment by playing at Red Indians. Older boys climbing a difficult rock face would see no merit or possibility of pleasure in departing from strict matter of fact. Two persons might be happy enough practising with racquet and ball against a rebound wall; it is likely, though not certain, that they would get increased pleasure if someone taught them to play squash. The varied merits and delights of games demand closer study. It is sufficient here to state a conviction that there is no merit without delight.

Recreation, Leisure and Sport
Physical education's concern with enjoyment is ultimately expressed in the belief that school physical education finds its natural continuance and to some extent its justification in post-school physical recreation and leisure time activity. The widespread use of the terms 'recreation' and 'leisure' in this context makes some examination of their meanings essential. They certainly do not mean the same thing.

Recreation seems to represent a more unified concept than leisure. The words 'recreation, recreative, recreational' are indistinguishable in meaning, except as parts of speech. 'Leisure, leisurely, at leisure' and 'leisure time' are much more loosely related. To do something 'at my leisure' may well refer to a job at the office which I reserve until the rest of the staff have gone home. The whole of the professional activities or indeed the life of some fortunate people may be described as leisurely. 'Leisure time' or 'leisure pursuits' come closer to recreation but still have a rather more elevated moral tone. 'Recreation' has a ring of pleasurable therapy about it. It is almost as though recreation—like medical treatment—becomes necessary because of a personal deficiency. The need may arise from a state of tension, stress or worry in which case the recreation will take on a relaxing, sedative form; or from a state of boredom and depression which will demand recreation as a stimulant. Leisure on the other hand seems related not so much to a need as to a duty. It may be related to a professional or social duty which makes the provision of sufficient leisure necessary, as in the case of a scholar, composer or poet. Or the leisure itself may be the fortunate circumstance of having time at one's disposal, and in this case there seems to be the feeling among civilised men that the time should be devoted to matters which are worthy of attention. There is no necessary connection between leisure and play or between leisure and enjoyment except—and this is important—that a man may be expected to enjoy a piece of activity, even a duty, which he performs without harassment or pressure. The idea of release from pressure as a characteristic of leisure slants the meaning of the word towards activities with a strong intellectual, creative or contemplative element; certainly not towards inactivity but towards activity which the performer is free to stand back from and savour as it happens. Highly competitive activities do not immediately spring to mind. Recreation, on the other hand, has come to be associated with fairly vigorous and not highly intellectual activity—witness our recreation grounds. It is interesting to speculate whether many people would consider the running of Roger Bannister on the evening of 6 May 1954, and in the weeks preceding, as either leisure or recreation.

Of course the concepts overlap. A man may fill the whole of his leisure time with recreation—and if he has very little leisure time he may well feel justified. Again many forms of activity which may, for certain people, have recreative, or even frankly therapeutic values, may, in their own right, satisfy even the highest standards regarding the spending of leisure time. Nevertheless it is possible to differentiate between the concepts and this differentiation (and indeed a certain gap which neither of them fills) will have some importance in our thinking about physical education as a source of pleasure.

Recreation refers to activity, often physically vigorous, possibly light-hearted or even frivolous on occasions, which justifies itself through the refreshment and personal satisfaction it brings to the performer. Leisure has a range of meaning but generally refers to a state of freedom from external pressure which enables an individual to use an extended period of time on matters which, for one reason or another, he feels worthy of his attention. The idea of the cultural value of leisure is strong. Neither concept will quite contain the activities of men like Bannister, Chichester or of any dedicated athlete. For them we need another concept, related to, but distinct from recreation and leisure. We need the concept of sport. This will accommodate a degree of concentration on standards of performance (often to the exclusion of any thought of its effect on the performer) which will mark it as more serious and more objective than recreation; and a degree of tension and competitive urgency which will bring it closer to combat than to leisure.

The enjoyment of continuing participation in physical activities after school age may therefore partake, in varying degrees, of the characteristic qualities we have identified. There may be the enjoyment of the creative and contemplative values inherent in the civilised use of leisure; there may be enjoyment of the striving for competitive excellence in sport; and there may be no more than the sheer fun of recreation. These three value areas will overlap but it would be well to recognise their separate identity. They will not apply equally to all men and women or to all boys and girls and this is a fact we must take into account when we come to consider the curriculum.

3: Quality in Movement: Skill

An examination of the two concepts of movement quality and skill is undertaken with the strong belief that these concepts will be found to come very close together, in fact so close as to constitute two aspects of the same thing.

The term 'movement quality' is sometimes used to designate a particular quality, for example strength or speed or delicacy, which a movement may possess. Such 'qualities' are all good qualities. Characteristics such as clumsiness or feebleness would not be referred to by the same term. In its more general sense, quality is often thought of in rather subjective terms as a characteristic of an aesthetic nature related to form and feeling rather than to function. In the present discussion the term 'quality' is used in a quite matter-of-fact way to represent the summation of all those characteristics which give value to a movement. It rests upon the idea that some movement is good and other movement is not so good; and the difference is referred to as one of quality. Quality is therefore very closely bound up with function, and, depending on the function, judgement of quality may, in varying degrees, be based on fact or opinion. To take an example from a more familiar context: it would be possible to assess the smoothness or the opaqueness of paper by purely objective tests, but whether the quality of paper is improved by smoothness or opaqueness would be, for some purposes, a matter of opinion. In the interests of precision it would be well to start our investigation by asking what are the various evaluative criteria by which actions and forms of movement may be judged. The following kinds of criteria suggest themselves:

(1) the degree and certainty of success in attaining the object of movement
(2) efficiency in the use of effort
(3) freedom from harmful postural habits and movement patterns
(4) beauty of form

In work, play or other rational activities the object of moving can generally be identified in one way or another. Sometimes it is difficult to achieve as in aiming a dart, threading a needle or striking a rapidly moving ball. Here objective success assumes great importance. Sometimes it is so easy to attain that it becomes almost meaningless as a criterion. Tasks of lifting and carrying, where no great load is involved and no great precision required, are tasks of this nature. Sometimes speed of performance with freedom from error becomes the criterion of success, as in typing. But there will be many examples of voluntary movement where objective success does not sufficiently discriminate.

The second criterion can be stated in purely mechanical terms: useful work done measured against energy expended. This applies in very heavy tasks, such as pushing a car, or tasks of an explosive nature such as performing a long jump, which will demand the skilful application of all available energy to produce the maximum effect. It also applies in lighter tasks, such as long-distance running, where the aim will be to use as little energy as possible. Performance which appears to economise in effort is often described as relaxed, and relaxation is commonly quoted as a main component of good movement. In all cases, whether the work rate is high or low, waste of effort through superfluous or ill-directed movement will reduce efficiency and must be considered as a sign of poor movement quality.

A point to bear in mind is that in some circumstances—say in dance or the expression of a mood of elation—it may be justifiable to be prodigal of effort, but these are exceptions with a rather unusual objective.

The practical possibility of applying the second criterion—like the first—will vary greatly in different situations. The advancing study of biomechanics may evolve techniques whereby objective assessment will be simplified and extended in range but it seems certain that, even where objective measures are applied, judgement of movement efficiency will, to a considerable extent, be subjectively based upon careful and understanding observation. This will be the province of the expert student of movement, trained in observation and versed in a wide variety of skills.

The first and second criteria of movement are commonly combined to constitute a definition of skill and the third criterion—the avoidance of harmful postural habits—calls for a kind of control which is certainly close to skill. The most common types of bad movement habits are those which place undue stress on joint mechanisms and those which induce unnecessary postural tensions in muscle groups. Joints can best be safeguarded by ensuring that weights are taken and stresses absorbed by stable skeletal structures or by adequate muscle masses rather than by unprotected connective tissue around joints. This is clearly an element in skill. It aids performance inasmuch as it prevents disability. In like manner the achievement of habits of postural relaxation appears to call for similar techniques and mental attitudes to the achievement of relaxation as an element of efficient performance. Informed and sensitive movement education may benefit health through skill.

It has been implied that, although voluntary movement must by definition have an objective of some kind, this is not always easy to identify. In dance and drama it may be the expression of a mood or an idea or the creation of an effect or an illusion. In social intercourse the same functions often hold, though less intensively developed. In situations of this kind, where the objectives of movements are psychological rather than material, evaluation will be in terms that are aesthetic or near-aesthetic in character. The value of a movement will lie in its observed form, whereas in movements with a material objective, form is associated with, but does not constitute the primary value. In movements where the value lies in the form, such as expressive or communicative movements, skill seems to play a rather special sort of role. It is the skill of the mimic artist. The movements are often not consciously learnt: they are 'picked up' by unconscious imitation. But this does not put them outside the realm of skill; after all, many highly skilled objective movements are picked up in the same way. And when the performer wishes to improve the quality of his expressive or communicative movement he must do it by a process of observation and practice in exactly the same way as he acquires a more physically objective skill.

The recognition of a movement quality which is purely aesthetic in nature will depend upon many complicated issues which merit detailed attention. Sometimes beauty is recognised in movement which is entirely artless, like the movement of a small child, or in functional movement where the sole object of attention is the task in hand. Only rarely, it seems, is beauty of form the conscious, primary aim in movement. Where it is, success would seem to depend not only on imagination and taste, but on the same sort of careful observation and control (even practice) as in movements with an operational or communicative function.

There is a further factor in movement, kinaesthetic satisfaction, which is of limited use as a criterion since it cannot be publicly observed. Like any other feeling it is difficult to identify and is sometimes misleading. But there seems to be a common agreement that free, unfatigued movement generally 'feels good' and that the total feeling whatever be its cause—physiological, psychological or both —is enhanced when there is accord between intention and performance.

From this discussion the idea presents itself that all learning in the field of movement quality (whether this is evaluated by ergonomic, hygienic or aesthetic standards) is a matter of the acquisition of appropriate skills.

The Concept of Skill

To give to skill a broad enough interpretation to fit this idea would not unduly stretch the meaning of the word. In common parlance it is even more broadly applied, since it covers intellectual as well as physical forms of activity. We talk of mathematical skill and skill in debate. If we narrow down the dictionary meaning by excluding these purely intellectual activities from our field of study, we may consider skill as coextensive with physical aptitude.

Some of the errors that physical educationists commonly make about skill arise from their failure to appreciate that, as Ryle[1] has reminded us: 'A skill is not an act; . . . it is a disposition'. Skill is a power over action; it implies an ability to act; but it is not an action. Though it may be convenient at times to refer to a performance as 'a skill', it should be remembered that this is only a figure of speech. Performance is evidence of skill and it forms the practice situation in which new skill is acquired. All skill is acquired through intelligent practice and each fresh acquisition of skill will be shaped by the practice situation from which it arose; but it will not be limited to

---

[1]Gilbert Ryle, *Concept of Mind*, 1949, p.33.

the precise form of this situation and it certainly must not be confused with it.

Skill involves a process of steering or psychophysical decision making; it implies a conscious motivation and an intelligent overcoming of difficulties. In this the idea of skill seems to coincide with the idea of competence: both depend upon a command of knowhow (the French use the verb *savoir* to denote the possession of purely physical skills). Conceptually both are independent of 'power' factors such as strength and endurance. One can succeed through strength or stamina and yet be lacking in skill. It has already been noted that degree of skill may be assessed either by the certainty or the speed of the action, by economy of effort or by the sheer excellence of the result. Though it is possible to imagine a person who has a particular skill without knowing it—who may agreeably surprise himself when he attempts a performance—in general, skill is consciously possessed. It is one of the outstanding features of the possession of skill, and one of its greatest values, that it carries with it the feeling of certainty, or at least of confidence, that one can perform satisfactorily. This confidence is based not merely on the external evidence of past successful performance but on the internal, mental image of the required performance. It is this mental content—always present even if the level of attention is low—which distinguishes skill from automatic responses like digesting a meal or reflex actions like removing the hand from a painfully hot surface. This mental grasp does not always involve an intellectual understanding of the mechanics or dynamics of the action, though it may. Some degree of such understanding would appear to be of value in facilitating the 'transfer' of skill from one task to another and in ensuring the permanence of skill or at least helping recovery of skill when it is lost. Ryle[1] distinguishes between 'habits' acquired through drill and 'intelligent capacities' acquired through more sophisticated forms of training like those of the doctor or the all-round mountaineer, whose very training demands that he should think. Ryle labels habits as 'automatic' and places them in a lower order. The difference is surely one of degree rather than kind. At the highest levels physical skill fuses with understanding and aesthetic

---

[1]Gilbert Ryle, *op. cit.*, p.42.

insight to produce masterpieces of construction or creative interpretation—like making a jewel or playing a sonata. At lower levels
the response is less consciously directed by the intellect but even at
the lowest levels it is hard to conceive of anything meriting the name
of skill which does not remain responsive, in some degree, to mental
control. This mental element in skill is important since it explains
skill's characteristic resilience and adaptability. No skill is absolutely
stereotyped; though a certain required form of action may be. The
term 'closed skill' is, strictly, a misnomer. It is the required response
which is closed, not the skill. Even in the most stereotyped circumstances, small changes will occur from time to time to which the
skill of the performer will characteristically adapt itself. The adaptability of skill is demonstrated from the very beginnings of its acquisition through practice. This is essentially a process in which a more
perfect performance arises out of a less perfect one. During learning,
performance is shaped by the image of what is being attempted as
well as by the memory of what has been achieved. There is no reason
to doubt that this power to adapt itself and extend its range will be
a permanent feature of any skill. But common experience demonstrates that extension of range is not infinite. Even with the most
versatile performer it is always possible to find a task where he will
fail through lack of experience. Take milking a cow. The truth must
be that in any situation a performer can only call on those particular
pieces of experience, simple or complex, which he happens to possess
and on such adjustments as he is able to make to them in the light
of his predication of any new circumstances in which he must act.
Since skill involves a process of decision making and decisions must
be made in advance of the contingency—if only momentarily—it is
indeed upon prediction (based on prior observation and continuing
through feedback during the action) that skill adjustment relies.
The competence to predict in this way, though it depends upon
intelligence and motivation, depends also upon experience and is
itself an aspect of skill. In situations where conditions are stable (the
draughtsman in his office) prediction is easy and does not assume
great significance. Where conditions change rapidly (car driving
or football) the accuracy of the prediction and the consequent adjustment of the habitual movement responses becomes of supreme
importance. This view of skill as subject to both external and internal

growth stimuli (depending essentially upon the accumulation of experiences but having its own inbuilt powers of adaptability and development under the intelligence and the will of the performer) seems to fit the well-known fact that high levels of skill manifest themselves neither as universal competence nor as rigid stimulus-response reactions; but rather as generalised facility within certain fields of behaviour. One person is good at managing horses, another at the use of joiner's tools, a third at football (or perhaps more generally at ball games), a fourth at dressmaking. These are four areas of skill which seem to have little contact with each other. It would be as wrong to think of a vast flood of indifferentiated aptitude as to think of a multitude of little skills in watertight compartments. Skill is like the power of thought. A thought merges with other thoughts: indeed it creates other thoughts. But facility in thinking will show itself in particular areas—mathematics, politics, physical science or engineering—in which practice has been obtained. Just as there is no conceptual distinction between individual thoughts and the process of thought, so there is no conceptual distinction between individual skills and the phenomenon of skill. The activity of the human mind in extending, adjusting and combining old skills to fit new circumstances demands the closest study both by researchers and by practising teachers. It is the facilitation of this process and its direction along useful channels which is the essence of good teaching. Through it the pupil may progress towards an integrated and versatile mastery of movement. Through it skills may become skill.

Movement: a general factor?

That physical education may confer a generalised competence—an appreciable degree of versatility—is a conviction widely held. Alexander Pope certainly took this as self-evident when he used it to illustrate a point he wished to make about writing.

> ' *True ease in writing comes from art, not chance,*
> *As those move easiest who have learnt to dance.* '

It is attractive, in any learning situation, to believe that what is learnt has a general significance and there have been various attempts to incorporate this idea into the theory and practice of physical education.

The most thoroughgoing theory is that movement itself is an art which can be mastered—that, by understanding certain principles and by learning to put into practice the fundamental elements of movement, a person can acquire a mastery which, at any rate in theory, can become complete. Laban and Lawrence,[1] writing about skill in the broadest possible context, assert that 'the best practical method consists of a combination of exercise and the awakening of the understanding of the rules of the proportionality between motion factors'. They identify these factors as weight, time and space together with a control of flow. This idea has found considerable acceptance in English physical education during the past quarter of a century. It has unquestionably produced some interesting and valuable effects in those types of activity where form and, to a lesser extent, feeling are used as criteria. Such types of activity are dance, mime, dramatic movement and the newer kinds of educational gymnastics. Form and feeling as criteria are achieved entirely within the person of the performer and it is to be expected that a method largely preoccupied with personal body awareness could be used with effect.

A distinction has already been suggested which may be of general interest. Some types of skilled activity depend entirely—and others extensively—on an ability to assume particular postural forms of movement. This is exemplified in dance and, even more strongly, in mime. This kind of skill may be said to involve a 'mimic' element since it seems to operate in response to a model, seen or imagined. The mimic artist can imitate the movements of the footballer, the weightlifter or the tight-rope walker, without the ball, weight or tight rope. This is the main material of mime. It is not the main material of dance (the dancer usually responds to models and formal concepts more related to the disciplines of his own art than imitative of movement in real life), but experience shows that the trained dancer can in practice reproduce required dynamic forms of all kinds, even direct imitations or caricatures, when called upon. So can other people to a greater or lesser extent. The ability undoubtedly depends upon a natural talent. Some children more readily than others reproduce the form of a movement which is shown or described to them. These may be the children we call good

---

[1]Rudolf Laban and F. C. Lawrence, *Effort*, 1947, p.7.

movers. But the talent just as obviously responds to training, particularly in movement observation. The training may take a variety of forms and may make use of a variety of ideas and a variety of terms (the idea of the integration of time, weight, space and flow is just one example). But, essentially, this kind of skilled performance is the outward reflection of an inner model. It may therefore be said (without any derogatory connotation) to have a mimic character.

The ability to reproduce movement forms is of great value in many situations, particularly those associated with expression or communication or with purely locomotor actions. In sport it produces the 'stylist'. But it is not the heart of the skill. The ability to make a flowing cricket stroke (such as many a dancer could make after a short period of initiation) would be of no value without the quite different ability to connect with a bouncing ball. In most operational situations the movement form is a secondary consideration. Form grows out of function. The attention is directed to critical parts of the environment, not to the body of the performer: to *what* he is doing rather than *how* he is doing it. There is no evidence to support the idea that a mastery of movement elements can confer any wide command of skill in this more functional field.

Less radical is the conception that one outcome of a comprehensive movement education may be the development of a general condition of motor sensitivity and competence which can be called 'movement sense',[1] in the way that a combination of sensitivity and competence in other fields may be called common sense, fashion sense or musical sense. This may be a useful idea and a useful term when used, like common sense, fashion sense or musical sense in a conventional context; or it may be more seriously regarded in relation to what has been called body concept. Body concept is held to be an integration of all the ideas and feelings one has about one's body. The notion appears to be that, starting from the purely spatial considerations of body extent, the concept enlarges to include ideas about what one's body can perform, what it can express and what it looks like. Individuals certainly do have ideas about themselves. These ideas seem to be more prominent in the consciousness of some

---

[1]See *Concept of Physical Education*, 'British Journal of Physical Education', Vol.I, No.4, July, 1970.

people than of others. They may be accurate ('the giftie gie us to see oursels as others see us'); they may be wildly extravagant or just wrong. They may produce a sense of self satisfaction, whether or not they are accurate, or they may be disturbing. Body concept, therefore, is a highly complex and highly individual affair. It becomes most obvious as a personal characteristic when it is erroneous or grotesque, as in the case of old Mr. Turveydrop in *Bleak House* who was obsessed with the idea of his own Deportment. In some of the modern tests,[1] where the criteria are those of satisfaction rather than accuracy, ridiculous old Mr. Turveydrop would get a high score for body concept. It is difficult to think of an integrated body concept for a man who knows himself to be rather inept on a dance floor or on a cricket field but supremely competent in a swimming pool or in the saddle of a horse. A person's legitimate idea of his physical adequacy to deal with events or to create an impression on other people—his body concept in other words—is likely to change radically from one environment to another. A feeling of confidence in relation to the problems of a particular environment has been identified as a characteristic of skill. Does not the development of body concept, therefore, like the acquisition of movement sense in the last analysis arise from 'a complex of skills reinforced by knowledge and favourable attitudes.'?[2]

A rather different attempt to identify a general effect in movement education involves the idea that 'movement behaviour' can be considered separately from other skill training.[3] This possibility deserves careful consideration. The term 'movement behaviour', or 'physical behaviour', is used to designate the total form of any individual's movements when engaged in the everyday performance of his personal and social functions. The most fundamental of these functions are those connected with locomotion, the simple manipulation of objects and communication with other persons. The movements of an individual when so engaged are a complex of maturational skills and acquired habits, some good, some bad, some indifferent. Since movements of this kind are constantly repeated

---

[1] See J. E. Kane, *Psychological Aspects of Physical Education and Sport*, p.96 (body cathexis).

[2] 'British Journal of Physical Education,' *op.cit.*

[3] *Op. cit.*, Some of the phraseology is repeated here.

and variously combined they may become fused into a single system of movement patterns which characterises the individual and is largely independent of the skills he has acquired for special purposes in work or play. As a new and better concept to put in the place of 'posture' it is clearly of importance from social, aesthetic and hygienic points of view and it is a concern which has always been attributed to physical education. Posture is not a concern with which we appear to have had any marked success and there is little interest in posture among physical educationists today. There is strong medical evidence that the teaching of postural relaxation is possible and valuable[1] and there is considerable public interest in the idea, as the popularity of Yoga testifies. There is nothing incompatible between this idea and educational gymnastics, but, should the interest in relaxation be re-developed within physical education, the approach in the gymnasium would surely be active and educative rather than therapeutic. Relaxation would be taught as an element of good movement, an element of central importance in the exercise of skill.

Warren Lamb[2] believes that the larger influences of the home and the school are more likely to be effective than instruction in the gymnasium. He writes: 'In the end we may find that the child who grows up with the highest standards of physical behaviour may do so because of environmental conditions and the influence of people with whom he is in contact, rather than because he attended dance or physical education classes, however up to date they may have been'. This expression of opinion is useful in emphasising the limitations of what physical education can do about movement behaviour but it will be harmful if it is taken by physical educationists as an excuse for doing nothing at all. Many people believe Pope was right about dance. Observation of individual dancers and groups of dancers, in normal domestic and social situations, seems to support the view that, on the whole, they do move better than most people. Perhaps only those who are inherently good movers can succeed at dance. Anyway, dance and good movement—poise, relaxation, deftness in manipulation and effectiveness in gesture—do seem to go

[1]See for instance C. H. Patel, *Yoga and Biofeedback in the Management of Hypertension.* 'The Lancet', 10 Nov., 1973.
[2]Warren Lamb, *Posture and Gesture*, 1965, p.109.

together, and, through the practice of dance, physical education may reasonably hope to exercise an influence on movement behaviour.

It is likely that physical education may exercise a similar influence through good teaching of normal locomotor skills, particularly in the early years. The qualities of fluency, poise and relaxation are key factors in locomotion, whether this is looked at as specific skill or, more generally, as movement behaviour. Beauty in movement will be considered in a later chapter, but, without further consideration at this point, it can be postulated that beauty in physical action will arise naturally from function. This contention is supported most strongly by the feeling we have that if a movement is ugly it must be wrong. People who believe that the action of a racing walker is ugly are likely to be those who believe that to walk at eight miles an hour is wrong. At that speed it is easier and more graceful to run.

So it seems that the pursuit of good movement is, in practice, the pursuit of skill; provided always that the pursuit is informed by a sensitivity and understanding that sees beauty of form and freedom from injury and stress as justifiable aims or valued attributes of skill; and provided also that the skill teaching is directed not only at the achievement of excellence in this or that activity but at range, versatility and general relevance. The achievement of excellence at specific tasks will, of course, be a matter of concern in physical education and this will be the aim of much of our skill teaching, but it is surely the interest in general relevance which will be the hallmark of the physical educationist as distinct from the athletic coach or dance instructor. He will attempt to achieve it in two ways: firstly by the attitude which inspires his teaching, by his catholicity of taste and interest and by his power to promote a general understanding of, and respect for, skilled performance of many kinds; and secondly by his care in prescribing a programme of activities which will not only be of value in their particular form but will contribute towards his pupils' overall skill equipment to face life. What should this overall skill equipment include? How far can the physical education programme contribute towards it? What other subjects have contributions to make? The physical educationist can only answer these questions in an enlightened way if he has made some attempt at a logical review of the total range of human skill.

¶ A CLASSIFICATION OF SKILLED ACTION

To classify the skilled actions observable in everyday life in any precise or comprehensive way, is virtually impossible. Actions are not organic wholes like birds, plants or even words. A simple action which will fit into one category of a classification, may, without losing its character, become rather more complex and qualify for inclusion in others. It is in the nature of skilled actions that they should be adaptable and should readily combine in the service of the human intelligence. The more complex they become the more interesting they are and the more difficult to classify. Yet, even at a complex level, some forms of activity are recognisably different from others. Embroidery, football and pheasant shooting are different in many ways; not least from the point of view of practice and learning, which carries with it their relationship to physical education.

A framework for a classification of skilled actions is given in the chart below. The various groups and sub-groups are such as appear to have some kinship in structure or quality which will be significant where learning is concerned. Such kinships can only be a matter of speculation until proved by experience. Physical educationists should not be lacking in suitable experience.

The classification deals only with single actions or unified forms of activity. It does not include organised games and other kinds of social behaviour which are artificial mixtures of many different forms of action. The relationship of these games and types of behaviour to the actions in the classification will demand specific study in every case.

The notes which follow the classification attempt to explain and develop the ideas upon which it is based.

CLASSIFICATION OF SKILLED PHYSICAL ACTION

Locomotion 1. *Personal*
- (i)   Pedestrian: walking, running, skipping, dance steps, sliding, jumping, simple vaults
- (ii)   Acrobatic: rolling, cartwheels, handwalking, somersaults, swinging, complex vaults
- (iii)   Climbing and high balance
- (iv)   Swimming

2. *Vehicular*
(i) Riding: cycling, skating, ski-ing, horse-riding, motor-cycling, parachuting
(ii) Piloting small vehicles: canoes, dinghies, toboggans, sports cars, gliders
(iii) Piloting large vehicles: lorries, launches, ships, aeroplanes, space craft

gradual change in character ↓

Operation 1. *Moving of objects*
(i) Delicate positioning: placing, fitting (dressing, eating at table), throwing (dart)
(ii) Vigorous propulsion: pushing, pulling, lifting, carrying, striking, kicking, throwing
(iii) Reaction to moving objects: catching, dodging, deflecting striking, kicking

2. *Constructive manipulation*
Infinite variety

Expression 1. *Sound*
(i) Bodily: clapping, stamping, whistling
(ii) Instrumental: percussion, wind, strings
(iii) Vocal: exclamation, speech, song

2. *Touch*
Handshake, caress, blow

3. *Gesture*
(i) Facial and bodily signs and signals
(ii) Gestural art forms (mime, dance)

Primary classification
Since the discussion deals with 'actions' and not 'movements', the primary classification is made on a basis of purpose and outcome rather than on movement form. A classification of 'movements' might have called for a category labelled 'postural movement'. There are undoubtedly many movements involving a change in body form—a change from one arrangement of trunk and limbs to another—without either locational change or environmental effect.

These could be called postural movements. But are they skills? Sometimes they are no more than a change of position to give muscular relief, like the stretch of the arms at an office desk or a change of position in bed. Sometimes they are artificially contrived callisthenic movements, significant rather as body training than as skills in their own right. Sometimes they involve taking up a position in relation to some operational task; in which case they should be considered as integral to the operation. Sometimes they relate to the conscious orientation of the body towards its total environment, like balance adjustment even in a position of virtual stillness. These must be considered as locomotor acts. After all, since locomotion involves the movement of the body from one position to another it does not seem unreasonable to include the positions as well as the movement. Standing is part of walking or jumping. Just as music includes both sound and silence, so locomotion can be considered as including both movement and stillness.

Locomotion
At quite an early age the infant strives to move from one place to another. When his parents first encourage him to roll by placing him free on a towel stretched on the floor his physical education (or, more specifically, his gymnastic training) can be said to have begun. From rolling he proceeds to crawling and later learns to walk. From this time onwards in his principal modes of locomotion he will be upright and balanced on his feet. He will walk, run and leap and will do little else. If he leads a very sheltered existence, without challenge or stimulation, even running and leaping will be restricted to a minimum. It is a particular responsibility of physical education to present challenge and stimulation, so that pedestrian forms of locomotion will be diversified and extended in range and other forms of locomotion will be introduced which the child might easily miss for lack of opportunity. The performance of dance steps has been included as locomotion. Though dance will justify itself on other grounds, it undoubtedly involves locomotor skills of a high order.

Playful or sporting types of locomotion which include the element of being 'upside-down' have been labelled acrobatic. Climbing actions often verge on the acrobatic but the really essential element in climbing skill seems to be 'a head for heights'. This is why balance walking has been grouped with the swarming type of climbing actions.

Swimming is different from any other from of locomotion. Man is not naturally adapted for swimming; he is 'out of his element'. For this very reason—involving the novel feeling of weightlessness when the art has been acquired—swimming is particularly enjoyable. This and its unique survival value give it a special significance.

All forms of locomotion demand control of speed and direction. In vehicular locomotion this factor assumes a special importance because of the development of an artificially high degree of momentum. The larger and more powerful the vehicle the greater the momentum is likely to be, and the more critical its control. But with large vehicles the individual actions of the pilot have an operational rather than a locomotor character. The vehicle is a machine which contains but is separate from the body of the pilot. He may even walk about inside it. In personal locomotion, on the other hand, every action is part of the locomotor process. The same is true when the performer is riding: the animal or apparatus (when properly ridden) is virtually an extension of the body of the performer. The control of a small vehicle retains something of this character.

Locomotor skills, particularly the personal and near-personal forms, are the heart of the physical education programme.

Operation

This covers an even wider and more heterogeneous category of action than locomotion. It includes all those actions through which a performer produces a physical effect outside his own body. This is the usual reason why man moves. Locomotion frequently subserves an operational aim.

Skilled work is normally done by the hands. The particular delicacy and precision of the human hand has given a rich meaning to the term manipulation. But even in strictly manipulatory actions the whole body is generally involved and in some quite complicated operational tasks (for example car-driving) the feet may play a prominent part. In very many tasks of this kind an implement, or even a machine is employed.

Delicate positioning

Tasks in this category are those which demand a high degree of motor control while presenting no problem about the development of force. The objects, characteristically, are small or delicately made. Sometimes they are thrown, but this is usually only for a recreative purpose, as in the games of darts or quoits. Some tasks such as tying up shoelaces are repeated so often that they become almost reflex, but usually where accuracy is required objects are carefully placed in position. It may be considered that for success in these actions care is the requisite rather than skill. Clumsiness is often no more than carelessness. But again it may be thought that the habit of taking care constitutes a certain form of skill.

Propulsion

These are actions in which the movement of an object demands the application of considerable force. Directional control may or may not also be of critical concern. Where it is, the direction as well as the magnitude of the force must be taken into account but the characteristic of the skill is the efficient use of the available strength resources of the performer either in an explosive act of impulsion or in the sustainment of the action over a long period. Such acts can be learnt.

There appear to be three distinguishable forms of action by which propulsive work can be done.

Firstly there is the action which is fundamental to human toil: the simple application of force through the hands, shoulder or other part of the body which is kept in contact with the object. Pulling, pushing, lifting and carrying (though these are not very precise terms*) seem to cover, between them, the variations of this form of action. In certain industrial and sporting contexts implements— notably levers and pulleys—are used to augment the force. The use of these implements often entails the adoption of an artificial or contrived form of force application with techniques of its own, as in scything or rowing a boat. But in all these actions the essential skill shows itself in a postural disposition towards the task which allows

---

*It is not always easy to distinguish between pulling and pushing. Carrying usually involves lifting. A lift may be a pull or a push.

the most effective use to be made of the large muscle groups and the performer's body weight.

Secondly, in striking and kicking, the force is developed as momentum in the hand, foot or implement and imparted to the object, with great impetus, as a blow. Kicking and striking are actions of an aggressive type which are still used in certain kinds of combat. Kicking is little used in civilised society apart from its use in football and some other games but striking, especially with an implement, features strongly, not only in games, but in industry and everyday life. It is frequently used to move an object a very short way against a very high resistance, as in driving a nail into wood or a stake into the ground.

Thirdly there is throwing, the action in which an increasing degree of momentum is imparted to an object which is released at an appropriate moment to follow the aim of the performer. Certain specific forms of striking, notably the golf stroke, illustrate the fact that the striking action contains a ballistic element which makes it akin to throwing; and the term 'throwing' is sometimes used with regard to certain tennis strokes. The simplest forms of throwing or tossing, as with a shovel, are no more than a freely accelerating pull-push action but the characteristic form of distance throwing with lighter objects is a specific learned action involving co-ordinated movements at the joints of wrist, elbow and shoulder. Many people never learn it. The ability to throw is an anthropoid characteristic. The lower animals can pull, push, carry, lift, strike and kick. Some can catch. Lacking hands they are never able to learn to throw.

Kicking, striking and throwing actions are staple items in the athletic repertoire. It seems reasonable to suppose that skill acquired through practice in physical education will have a fairly general value. In common experience only a limited range of objects is subjected to these actions. For instance having learnt to throw a quoit, a cricket ball, a basketball, a rugby ball, a javelin and a shot, one may, with justification, feel one has fairly completely mastered the art of throwing. Industrial striking skills (primarily with hammers) are somewhat outside the range of the normal athletic programme and the skills involved in pushing, pulling, lifting and carrying certainly do not enjoy a comprehensive coverage. There is everything to be said for their systematic inclusion in more work-orientated periods of training in the gymnasium.

Reaction to Moving Objects

Actions in this category demand the ability to predict the paths of objects moving freely in the environment. The characteristic task is one in which the action itself is not difficult to perform: the skill appears in the accuracy with which the action is informed by judgement of the speed, direction and momentum of the moving object. When an object is moving at high speed, on a parabola under gravity or rebounding from an interposed surface, a high degree of predictive judgement may be required: and the performer is faced with further complications when more than one moving object is involved. The skills may be those of interception (catching), avoidance (dodging) or alteration of course of an object already in motion (deflection). In all these skills the judgement of the movement path is predictive. Action must be initiated well in advance of the arrival of the moving object at the point where action is effective. This is particularly obvious at squash, where a player often begins to move into position to meet a ball at a time when it is moving away from him.

Apart from their practical utility, skilled actions of this kind are highly spectacular and uniquely satisfying as physical experience. All values are augmented when these skills are combined with various forms of locomotion and the human body itself becomes a moving object.

Physical education provides ample experience of activity of this kind. Indeed it could be maintained that nowhere else, outside the circus training school, is experience provided so richly as in ball games and their appropriate practices.

Constructive Manipulation

Most constructive actions are complexes of simple propulsive movements but the attention of the performer is directed at effecting some change of form in the material worked on. This effect is unique to the action. The forms of lifting and pushing used by the plasterer are special to his skill. So are those of the pastrycook. Each action depends upon a critical and specific relationship between the mover and his material.

Constructive action may be performed with the hands or with an implement. Many actions, such as sewing or carving or writing, cannot be performed without an implement. Machines such as sewing machines or lathes can extend the constructive capacity of the human hand and often make high manipulatory demands. But machines which are purely automatic, requiring no more than starting and stopping, hardly come within the bounds of this discussion.

Construction embraces the largest and perhaps the most important category of human skills. Each skill can be acquired only by bona fide practice. There seems little that physical education can contribute. A wide experience of the arts and crafts can do more.

Expression

Physical expression may be thought of as any movement, voluntary or involuntary, which makes apparent an intention, an idea or an inner mental state. Where there is a recipient, expression becomes a form of communication: though this communication, again, may or may not be deliberate. A man may make an expressive movement—he may even dance—when he is alone, or when he thinks he is alone. It is where an action is deliberately communicative that the idea of skill is most strongly developed.

The physical skills involved in the production of sounds are capable of reaching a high degree of sophistication since they become related either to the art of music or, through speech, with the physical expression of human thought and feeling. In discussing the connections between intellectual and physical activity A. N. Whitehead ranks the voice as one of the focusing points, along with the eyes, the ears and the hands.

Tactile expression of intent or feeling is by social convention, used only in rather limited circumstances. A nudge is considered vulgar; a pat on the back or a restraining hand is likely to be resented as an interference. Beyond the conventional handshake, tactile communication, doubtless because of its immediacy and its great evocative power, is generally considered permissible only in a context of well-established personal intimacy.

Visual communication of states of mind may be effected through movement at various levels of deliberation. At the lowest level are the involuntary starts, changes of tension or changes of position which are better ranked with eye dilation, pallor and blushing, as signs of emotion rather than as expressive action.

One way in which true expressive action can operate is through mutual experience of some form of organised physical activity with an understood content and method. Gymnastics, games and dance all provide examples of this. The initiated enjoy a fellow feeling based on the ability to appreciate points of significance, without explanation, as they occur. The communicative power here lies in the form of the activity itself. The game becomes a language. In the same way, music, a work of architecture, or even an internal combustion engine can constitute a centre of interest among a knowledgeable group and provide a means for the communication of ideas even without the aid of words. Further than this, in games and athletics the strongly conative, often competitive, nature of the activities encourages personal action among the performers which is expressive of feeling, motive or intention. In the heat of the contest expressive quality is usually unintentional. When a footballer works his way towards goal he is not usually intending to express or communicate anything. Nevertheless his actions may be highly expressive—of aggression, deliberation, confidence or cunning. The expressiveness of skilled action is of great significance to the observer. But it is something quite distinct from the skill which is expressive in intent. When the footballer turns and leaps delightedly in the air, when he calms the tempers of his colleagues with a movement of his hands, when he expresses regret and apology with a different movement or when he tricks an opponent by a feint, he is performing actions which are expressive in effect and in purpose. This is true gesture.

The use of gesture may be either in place of, or in amplification of verbal language. The strength of gesture (and facial expression) is its immediacy and its power. Its deficiency, when it supersedes or unduly overshadows verbal discourse, is its lack of precision and refinement of meaning. Demagogues may turn both this strength and this deficiency to their advantage. In public speaking and on the stage, as in social life, the use of gesture is very much a matter of taste. Gestures easily become habitual and are often not consciously controlled but, even as a habit, gesture embodies the personality, that is the mind. It is nearer to a skill than to a reflex.

What can education, and in particular physical education, do about this? The answer must to some extent be the same as that given in the case of posture or movement behaviour, since gesture must be considered as part of this complex of habitual action patterns. The child will learn by contact, by imitation of what he feels to be attractive or socially acceptable rather than by attention to precept. Direct teaching is, in any case, almost impossible in the absence of accepted norms. Such advice and correction as is given— generally in the family—is based more on taste (or prejudice) than on principle. It is, to say the least, doubtful whether instruction in the everyday use and abuse of gesture could be organised widely as curricular activity. What can be undertaken is a formal study of expressive skill in the context of dance and in mime. Beyond this, physical education seems to offer good opportunities for discipline in the control of socially undesirable forms and degrees of expression— or exhibitionism—and (not unrelated to this discipline) a recognition that good functional movement has an eloquence of its own.

Skill and Learning : Recapitulation

Skill can be thought of as a form of knowledge. Skilled actions are examples of the use of that knowledge. The range of useful application to which any particular new piece of knowledge can be put will depend upon (a) the nature of that piece of knowledge and (b) the intelligence and interest of the learner. Pieces of knowledge which are merely committed to memory and used in a stereotyped way by many a modern schoolboy were, to Pythagoras or Newton, the starting points for whole systems of thought. Our state of receptivity, our interest, our need, helps to determine not only how quickly we acquire knowledge but how widely and how effectively we apply it. It is the same with skill.

'Transfer of training' is a concept invented by experimental psychologists to represent a demonstrable relationship between a piece of training for a specified task and standard of performance at some other task. Transfer represents range in the use of skill. The concept of positive transfer implies that one skill—or organised group of skills—can be used with advantage in more than one situation. Sometimes transfer is found to be positive; sometimes it is nil and sometimes it is negative, where one skill interferes with another.

This last is interesting as showing the dangers of too mechanistic a view of transfer. If the degree of transfer were purely dependent upon the respective natures of the two tasks (as in a chemical reaction) one would expect positive and negative transfers to be equally likely to occur and equally powerful when they do. But, in normal life, negative transfer seems to be comparatively rare and, experimentally, as Holding[1] points out, it is usually so weak and so temporary as to be of no more than academic interest. This highlights the existence of the other factor in the operation of transfer— the human intelligence. People do not *want* one skill to interfere with another, so they see to it that interference is eliminated. The same factor—intelligent motivation—will fortify positive transfer. Its strength will vary between individuals. With some it may well overshadow in importance the precise material of the learning situation—the aptness of the practice and the skill of the teacher.

Nevertheless it can be reliably shown that transfer operates more strongly between some skilled actions than between others. Clearly this must be due to characteristics of the actions themselves—similarities, differences or relationships of some kind or other. The nature of these relationships is a matter of speculation.

It is often stated nowadays that 'skill is specific'. The statement has no real meaning until we are told what skill is specific to. It is certainly not specific to the precise action through which it was acquired. Whiting[2] explains: 'The specificity of skilled behaviour means that if success is to be obtained in a particular skill area extended practice in that area is a pre-requisite'. This is a reasonable statement and probably as near the truth as we can get in this complex matter. But what is an area of skill? Whenever transfer is shown to take place between two skilled actions it could be held to follow that they are in the same skill area. Holding[3] makes the interesting suggestion of two rather different principles which contribute to positive transfer. The first, which he calls 'inclusion', seems to tie up with the idea of skill areas; the second, 'performance standards' introduces other ideas. (He applies these principles only to the matter of transfer between an easy and a

---

[1] D. H. Holding, *Principles of Training*, 1965, p.109.
[2] H. T. A. Whiting, *Acquiring Ball Skill*, 1969, p.viii.
[3] D. H. Holding, *op. cit.*, p.114.

difficult task, but they seem relevant whatever the degree of difficulty involved.) One task, Holding points out, may include another task: 'After practising to shoot at an apple no further practice is necessary to hit a barn door'. Holding goes no further than this but he would surely agree that, without the complete inclusion of one task in another, there may be elements in common. Learning to ride a motor cycle is easy if you can already ride a bicycle and drive a car. This is certainly a most important factor in the purely mechanistic aspects of transfer. The elements which are transferred are virtually identical competences. But this explains only part of the matter, as Holding's second principle indicates.

By 'performance standards' he has in mind all those tendencies, habits and attitudes which the particular nature of one task may encourage and which may then transfer to another. He instances the tendency to prefer accuracy to speed which may be encouraged where the initial task is not too difficult. Transfer effects depend, says Holding, upon 'the outcome which is favoured'. In other words they are subject to intelligent decision-making on the part of the performer. This brings us close to the idea of the 'transfer of principles', though, as Holding points out, it is a matter of choice whether we regard, say, speed habits as a principle or as an 'abstract characteristic of a response'.

Experimenters report that transfer in physical education activities, appears to decrease as the child grows older. This is as one would expect. When a young child first learns to hit a moving ball with an implement, a whole world of skilled performance opens up to him. The skill will rapidly transfer to tasks involving all sorts of balls and all sorts of implements—and probably beyond that. There is *room* for transfer. But a new ball skill acquired by a child of fifteen is not likely to open up such wide possibilities. Any transfer is likely to be obscured by the fact that a wide range of ball skills has already been mastered. The more sophisticated and highly charged we become—in skill or other forms of knowledge—the less likely it is that a new piece of learning will have a wide-ranging effect. But as long as we are capable of learning at all, the possibility is surely there.

With young children we should have general values in mind. We would not expect the acquisition of ball skills to help them to climb, or climbing to help them to swim so we must devise a programme which includes these and many other kinds of things. But within this wide programme we would expect skills to fuse in mutual reinforcement. Even ball skills, climbing and swimming might—from the point of view of personal attitudes—reinforce one another. The teacher of physical education should continually look for opportunities to foster such reinforcement whenever it appears.

4: Beauty

Even the most prosaic of persons, whether participant or observer, must at times encounter the feeling that human movement, in addition to any functional justification has independent value on the grounds of beauty. Physical education certainly draws strength from this and at the present time theorists are busily engaged in formulating what in the past has been a vague, if warmly held, intuition into a serious claim to aesthetic significance.

There are two levels at which this claim can be stated. Firstly there is the point of view expressed by some members of our profession who talk of the 'art of movement' or of 'movement as an art form'. Their attention is really centred on dance; and the orthodox idea, nowadays, is that since dance is one of the established arts, dance in schools (though under the physical education umbrella) must be regarded as part of aesthetic education. This idea will be considered in a later chapter. The second viewpoint is commonly expressed without the use of the word 'art' and certainly without any claim for consideration as aesthetic education. It is simply that good movement is, in some way not generally understood, beautiful movement. It will be the aim of this chapter to examine this second point of view.

The field of Aesthetics is a fascinating but dangerous field for the amateur, consisting, as it does, of a vast literature supporting a not very well organised branch of philosophy. The views of the professional philosopher[1] have been typically expressed: 'Aesthetics presupposes part of moral philosophy, moral philosophy presupposes philosophy of mind, philosophy of mind presupposes metaphysics and metaphysics logic—so if you pick up something near the end of the chain you're in for the earlier parts too'. In the face of this rather

---

[1]Anon

daunting proposition comfort can be found in R. G. Collingwood's[1] estimate of the real, if limited, virtues of the artist as against the philosopher in the role of aesthetician. The artist knows what he is talking about; he is discriminating; he can recognise beauty even if he has a tendency to talk nonsense about it. As artists, or practitioners, in the field of human movement, physical educationists can surely lay claim to powers of discrimination. On this assumption the discussion which follows will concern itself with an attempt to identify the qualities which characterise beautiful movement rather than to engage in speculation or to propound a theory. But even for this limited task it will be necessary first to make certain comments about the nature of beauty and the importance of taste.

The Idea of Beauty

Some writers, Dewey and Santayana amongst them, believe that aesthetic experience is quite common in human beings, as, in the course of their everyday activity, they recognise comeliness and fitness of form in objects and events around them. Such experience, these theorists believe, is refined and intensified, but is not different in kind, where works of high art are concerned. Berenson, Clive Bell and other writers believe that art only exists in relation to a special class of human works which possess 'significant form.' Whatever view is taken on this matter, aestheticians and lexicographers seem to agree that beauty is a quality which may or may not appear in a work of art and which can exist—for instance in nature—quite independently of art. Beauty appears to be accepted as a more homely quality and much more universally apprehended than art. Clear thinking on this matter is not helped by the fact that the adjective 'aesthetic' is used in connection both with beauty and with art: and there is certainly divergence of opinion about the 'purity' with which beauty can be observed. G. E. Moore[2] takes a rigorous line. He writes 'When I speak of the cognition of a beautiful object . . . I must be understood to mean only the cognition of the beautiful qualities possessed by that object and not the cognition of other qualities of the object possessing them'. He maintains further that even the cognition of these essential aesthetic qualities

[1]R. G. Collingwood, *Principles of Art*, 1937, p.3.
[2]G. E. Moore, *Principia Ethica*, 1903, p.115(2).

will not, of itself, constitute 'seeing the beauty'. 'Seeing' involves more than understanding: it involves appropriate emotion. Other writers view such analysis with distrust. Eric Newton[1] writes 'there is no such thing as a "pure" experience. . . . However inconvenient it may be to have to admit it, the sense of sight is only one factor in our estimate of what is visibly beautiful. . . . Unconsciously we combine the visual image with perceptions independently provided by other senses into a *single emotional attitude*'.

Most people would probably not agree with R. G. Collingwood[2] in his wish to use the word 'beautiful,' like *'kalos'* in Greek, as applying to anything—from whatever cause—considered attractive or desirable; but beauty, unlike art, is generally understood as something which gives unmixed pleasure. The words 'balance', 'harmony', 'grace' and 'proportion' which frequently appear as central terms in definitions of beauty are all terms which not only relate to pleasurable sensation but represent concepts which the layman will view with understanding and sympathy.

One factor which will undoubtedly influence any discussion of beauty in human movement is the relation between beauty and function. This is not a simple relationship. Many supremely beautiful things have no function. Occasionally, one is told, a beautiful vessel or implement functions badly; but it never *looks* as though it will function badly. If it does we are hardly likely to think of it as completely beautiful, even though it may have beautiful features, say in texture or decoration. When we come across an ugly thing which functions successfully or which pleases us in some other way, we are rather puzzled. The orbiting spaceman, relieved to see the approach of the returning moon landing craft, was heard to say 'How come you look so good when you're so ugly?' The truth seems to be that we expect an object—or a movement—that functions well to be visually pleasing: and we are puzzled when it is not. Berkeley[3] writes: 'The beauty . . . of a chair cannot be apprehended but by knowing its use, and comparing its figure with that use; which cannot be done by the eye alone, but is the effect of judgement'.

---

[1]Eric Newton, *Meaning of Beauty*, 1950, pp.54-57. (slightly re-arranged quotation).
[2]R. G. Collingwood, *op. cit.*, p.38.
[3]Berkeley, *New Alciphron*, iii, 8

Taste

Discussing the criterion of taste, George Santayana[1] wrote: 'Dogmatism in matters of taste has the same status as dogmatism in other spheres. It is initially justified by sincerity, being a systematic expression of man's preferences, but it is absurd when it pretends to have absolute scope. . . . Taste is bound to maintain its preferences but free to rationalise them. After a man has compared his feelings with the no less legitimate feelings of other creatures he can reassert his own with more complete authority. . . . Reflection refines particular sentiments by bringing them into sympathy with all rational life. There is consequently the greatest possible difference in authority between taste and taste. . . . High water marks of aesthetic life may easily be reached under tutelage. . . . What painters say about painting and poets about poetry is better than lay opinion. . . . Good taste comes from experience'.

The recognition of beauty in movement, like beauty in anything else, will be a matter of taste, but taste can be cultivated 'under tutelage'. Should not such tutelage, where human movement is concerned be provided by those who profess and practise the arts of human movement, by athletes and dancers and physical educators?

Taste is sometimes used as another word for fashion. Taste, or fashion, in movement will certainly vary from generation to generation and from one cultural group to another—particularly when movement is considered as a social grace or a means of expression. Such variations are likely to show themselves as reflexions of social and moral attitudes. This is a fascinating field of study, in which the physical educationist, dancer or other student of movement might well collaborate usefully with the anthropologist or the social historian.

Beauty in Movement

The foregoing discussion, and especially the disclaimer of any intention of becoming involved in matters concerning forms of art, may be felt to justify the use of the word beauty with its popular connotation—as a quality, or combination of qualities, in the visual

---

[1] George Santayana, *Life of Reason*, One-Volume Edn., 1954, pp.367-71.

form of an object or event which attracts and holds the attention, gives pleasure and rewards contemplation. It will be assumed that, though it occurs through vision of the external form, the apprehension of beauty will be influenced by the observer's experience and judgement in relation to what he recognises to be the nature and purpose of the object or event observed.

An important consideration that will influence the whole question of beauty in movement is that the human body, as such, is generally thought to be attractive in form. Though, as somebody has pertinently observed, the ideal of human beauty is by no means the average specimen, there is among human beings, as among other animals, a feeling of attraction towards, rather than repulsion from, the external form with which nature has endowed their species. In this connection it may be of value to point out that human movement is really an abstraction. By discipline and training one may acquire the art of making a formal assessment of this abstraction but what is actually seen is not human movement but a particular human body in movement. He would be a very severe and academic observer who would claim that his assessment of a movement was unaffected by the shape of the mover.

Movement as Expression

The beauty of human movement may in certain circumstances, and by certain observers, be seen and appreciated in purely formal terms like the beauty of a work of architecture or other non-representational art. It is much more likely that formal appreciation will be mingled with ideas, moods, feelings and attitudes which the movement appears to express or embody.

This is an area of experience which is not only highly personal but carries moral as well as aesthetic overtones. It has been pointed out (page 42) that, viewed as a means of expression or communication, movement, though powerful, is unsuited to the expression of precise or complicated ideas. There are, of course, certain elemental gestures (more powerful if combined with facial expression) which convey fairly generally understood meanings. Gestures of aggression, surprise and conciliation and a whole range of gestures to open or close discussion of a matter (gestures in which the palms of the hands play such an important part) are now the stock-in-trade of

the professional footballer. Such gestures usually have a strong
natural potency, related to the functions of hands, head, chest and
abdomen, which transcends the barriers of class and language,
though the use of particular gestures is sometimes culturally circum-
scribed. Tolstoy mentions a gesture—a tilting of the head from side
to side to express bewilderment—which is habitual only among the
Russian people.

Mention has already been made of expressive skill. In a consideration of expressive beauty many of the same ideas will present themselves but a difference may be felt in that beauty, unlike skill, implies a certain degree of approval. Beauty implies liking and it is
hard to like a thing without approving of it. A movement—say a
gesture—which is wholly cowardly or wholly cruel may be recognised as skilful but it will not be aesthetically pleasing. This is
brought out by Theodor Lipps[1] in his postulation of what he calls
Einfühlung or empathy. He wrote: 'I see a man making powerful,
free, light, perhaps courageous motions of some kind, which are
objects of my full attention. I feel a sense of effort . . . with my feeling
of activity I am absolutely incorporated in the moving body . . .
This is . . . aesthetic empathy'. It is clear that in the example Lipps
feels moral approval of the movements described. They are more
than seen; they are felt to be good. It would be difficult to carry on
such a discussion in relation to formal beauty alone.

In a later work Lipps[2] does carry on the discussion and on clearly
moral grounds. He distinguishes between the positive empathy with
a gesture of noble pride and the negative empathy with one of
foolish vanity. 'I am aware of the noble pride as an affirmation of
vitality which I gladly embrace, of the foolish vanity as something
repulsive because it is the negative of vitality. . . . Both are experienced, the one as a free activity . . . the other as an oppression'.

Aesthetic empathy may be felt with gesture (movement purely
expressive in character) or with functional movement. The nurse
who is entirely engrossed in treating an injury may express solicitude
by her actions as surely as does the bystander who makes a gesture
of sympathy. And one cannot help feeling that the ties with function
provide a range and discipline which may add power and sincerity

---

[1] E. F. Carritt, *Philosophies of Beauty*, Oxford, 1931, (translations from Lipps) p.253.
[2] *Op. cit.*, p.257.

to the expression. The conscious use of gesture can be learnt and sometimes used with good effect but the effect will certainly be greater if the gesture appears to be unstudied. This probably explains why, in civilised society, what is cultivated more generally than expressive gesture is the habit of restraint which reduces gesture to a conventional level. On the whole most of us would prefer to be thought of as undemonstrative than the reverse. Whether in this country we have carried this preference to the point where it constitutes a denial of human sympathy is as much a moral as an aesthetic question.

Elements of Beauty in Movement
Since beauty of any kind will, in the last resort, be a matter of taste and since it will almost always arise from an inspired or fortunate combination among many elements (and since, furthermore, beauty in movement is so intimately bound up with functional and moral considerations) it appears unlikely that it will submit to any formal analysis. In this discussion nothing more will be attempted than the identification of certain qualities which can be visibly recognised in human movement and which may be useful in the examination of a particular movement from an aesthetic point of view.

The following qualities are suggested:

Fluency   Balance
Rhythm   Style
Power

Clearly these are not the only terms in which movement can be evaluated from an aesthetic point of view. The critic of movement, like the critic of art or music, will be free to choose his own terms and he has the whole language to choose from. The qualities, as listed, are conceptually distinct from each other but they fuse in performance and, in fusion, may suggest the use of other terms. For instance a movement which manifests a high degree of fluency, power and dynamic balance might be called agile. Agility in movement is certainly an attractive quality.

It goes without saying that skill is necessary for the realisation of all and every quality enumerated. Skill is an all-pervading quality rather than one to be listed on its own account.

Harmony is a term often used in connexion with aesthetic appraisal of movement, particularly dance. Choreographic artists talk of harmonic relationships in near-technical terms. For the uninitiated observer, harmony, like skill, is a general rather than a particular quality. It is through a harmonious (rather than harmonic) relationship that the various aspects, phases and formal attributes of a movement combine into a satisfying whole.

Fluency

Fluency, or flowing quality, in a movement, or between one movement and another shows itself in the way necessary changes in speed or direction are negotiated. Fluency demands that all such changes should be smooth, that sudden stops and starts should be avoided and, above all, that there should be no hesitancy or lack of drive. For though fluency involves flexibility—and may be marred by articular disfunction—it involves more than aimless flexibility. There is an impression of freedom but not of aimless freedom. The essential impression is that onward purposeful impetus is retained. In many functional movements, such as those of the coal heaver or the discus thrower, there is indeed a ballistic element depending upon physical momentum. This is generated, developed, conserved and utilised in a movement which follows a characteristically flowing pattern. There are other movements which have a flowing shape but in which there is no appreciable forward impulse. The movement is on a tight rein. The limb is carried, not thrown. It can be speeded up, slowed down or stopped at will. And yet it retains the fluent shape of a ballistic action. This is Rudolf Laban's 'bound flow'. He explains the phenomenon by postulating that fluency is, in fact, a sensation within the mover, which may continue during 'bound flow' or even during a pause.[1] This probably corresponds with the experience of persons using this type of movement which mainly seems to be connected with expressive forms of activity of one kind or another. In various epochs it has been fashionable in polite society as an adornment. It may appear in the expansive gesture of an orator. It is extensively used in dance and often in other performing arts. A perfect example is provided by the pianist who lifts his hands and lowers them again to the keys with a slow, unbroken flowing movement. He would most probably claim that his movement is

---

[1]Rudolf Laban, *Mastery of Movement*, 1960, p.8.

not in any way an adornment but an essential embodiment of his feeling and a technical aid in the judgement of rhythm and touch.

The distinction between free and 'bound' flow is not absolute. The movements of the pianist or the dancer may change imperceptibly between free and 'bound'. And in the freest of skilled movements there are strong elements of control operating all the time. The extreme flexibility of the human framework, which makes fluency possible also makes some joint fixation essential for the maintenance of form. Changes in speed and direction can only be effected—no matter how smoothly—against a physical background resistance which involves muscular tension and often involves a fixed and immovable base of support. This is brought out strikingly in the mechanics of the normal walking stride. Simple locomotion can be effected by a reaction between the hip joints and the points of contact with the ground. This is what happens in stilt walking and the result is anything but fluent. There is a series of start-stop actions where, at every step, new muscular and gravitational impetus is needed to get the body's weight centre over the next hump in its path. In normal walking the cushioning effect of the heel-toe transfer and the smoothing action of the knee extensors (lengthening and shortening but always active) combine to produce the wave-like, 'roller-coaster' motion of the body mass so easily observed in a regiment of marching men. Yet the points of contact with the ground are as firmly fixed and the course of the movement is as firmly controlled as in the 'unfluent' action of stilt walking. In many vigorous movements, both in athletics and everyday life, changes in direction and changes of speed may be much more rapid and sudden than those in walking. Examples of such movements are the take-off of the high jumper and the final stamp of the shot putter. Here it is necessary for the element of rigidity to assert itself strongly in order that the other element—onward impetus of the essential moving points—can be maintained. Both elements contribute to the quality of fluency. The smoothing mechanisms add to efficiency; without them many of our common skills, such as running, would be impossible; and they surely will be allowed as adding to the beauty of human locomotion.

Staccato movements may be used for dramatic effect; but in normal life stiff postures and halting movements are taken as the signs of injury, uncertainty, or lack of skill. Fluency implies competence, purpose and discipline. It is likely to appear in the movements of the expert rather than those of the novice; in the movements of the well co-ordinated adult rather than those of the small child.

Rhythm

Rhythm is an aesthetic value perceived in variations of sequential emphasis. The sequence in question may be an extended arrangement of shapes or a series of events. Rhythm will be recognised as an unfolding pattern compounded of (a) the intensity or degree of particular qualities (height, colour, pace, loudness, pitch) which serve to mark certain features in a sequence and (b) spatial or temporal relationships between these features as they appear. To form such a pattern the variations in emphasis must contain an element of repetition.

Rhythm helps to give cohesion to any sequence of shapes or events in which it is recognised and in some forms of continuous activity, say the beating of a drum, rhythm itself may be the dominant factor in the structure of the whole activity. Rhythm is an essential element in music, poetry and dance. It may be simple or complex, insistent or elusive but in these forms of art the aesthetic significance of sequential emphasis is fundamental. Rhythm is sometimes recognised in other arts, particularly those involving a design over which the eye of the beholder may be expected to travel, and rhythm may also appear in the experiencing of everyday sounds, sights and movements which are not organised into art forms. Since rhythm is a qualitative concept its effects can never be prejudged. Rhythms will vary and tastes will vary. But there can be little doubt that the recognition of a rhythmic element in a human physical action can, and usually does, increase its attractiveness. The rhythm in the run-up of a bowler immediately springs to mind.

Rhythm and fluency are distinct qualities which are not always present together in a movement but, where they are, they cannot fail to integrate with each other into what will appear as rhythmic fluency or fluent rhythm.

Power

Lipps, in his example of movement which inspires positive empathy quotes power before any other quality. The idea of power and the evidence of power arouse admiration because they are symbols of vitality. The beauty of power in movement lies in its being completely adequate for the task in hand. It is recognised through directness and confidence in approach and through firmness and ease in performance. It is destroyed by any sense of strain or loss of poise. It may appear in the positive actions of a woman ironing linen as well as in the fluent lifting efforts of the foundry worker or in the instant, free and rapidly accelerating motion of the great runner.

Balance

The preserving of equilibrium gives dignity to a movement; the endangering of equilibrium gives it excitement. In a slow, stately movement, character and quality show themselves through the constant preserving of a finely controlled equilibrium. The performer is never, even momentarily, off balance more than is necessary for essential locomotion. Contrastingly, in the fast, adventurous movements of gymnastics, dance and athletics, equilibrium is alternately imperilled and saved from second to second.

A person will not willingly 'lose his feet' except for a very special reason. A fall is usually accidental or a sign of failure. A somersault in gymnastics or a falling movement in dance will normally continue into a regaining of the feet (except for comic effect which has its own aesthetic). In sport there are occasional demands for a single self-justifying movement involving a fall—such as a goalkeeper's dive to save or a rugby player's dive to score. These may be among the most spectacularly beautiful movements in sport and they seem to demand an effective control of balance as a prerequisite to successful performance.

Control of equilibrium which is precise and confident, where there is no uncertainty or too-obvious adjustment, no recourse to extraneous aids or enlarged bases of support—where the base of support may be as small as the tumbler's hands or the ballerina's toe—this certainly is a quality in movement which most observers will recognise as an element of beauty.

Beauty in movement merges with beauty in stillness. It is in stillness or slow movement that it becomes most apparent that postural beauty involves more than mechanical stability. Stability can be facilitated, and frequently is facilitated, by the adoption of a crouching position but, aesthetically, it seems there is a certain human value in an upright posture. Though rules for posture are much less confidently stated than they were, there appears to be general approval for a position of balanced uprightness.

Style

Style implies refinement in conformity with cultivated standards of taste. It is therefore a social as well as an aesthetic consideration. In uncultivated societies or states of society beauty may show itself but not usually anything that would be called elegance or style. Elegance or style seems to demand conscious study and application to achieve a certain aesthetic effect. Paradoxically the effect is usually characterised by a minimal display of effort.

In operational or athletic forms of activity the acknowledged experts are the judges of style. Canons of style are normally related to supposed functional values but a stylish performer is not necessarily more effective than an unstylish one; he merely conforms more nearly with the aesthetic consensus. In everyday social activity the connexion between style and function is even slighter. Some basis of rationality may be found in the idea that civilised conventions (for instance the way one closes a door or uses a soup spoon) equate with good manners in expressing consideration for the feelings of other people. And even where other people are not directly involved, movements may still express a civilised attitude of mind. When D. H. Lawrence writes of 'pure fine movement even if only putting a book on a shelf' he may have in mind a movement which embodies a certain attitude towards books and shelves: but, more likely, he means that the movements, like the speech, of a civilised person should be characterised by a clarity of form which has its own aesthetic justification, irrespective of expressive or functional effects. This is very clearly seen in a consideration of the manner in which a person walks.

Style, in the abstract, may at times become fused with the practice of a particular style. Here aesthetic appreciation will depend upon knowledge, experience and the cultivation of taste in relation to that style. One thing is certain. A mixture of styles is likely to be unpleasing. To take an extreme example, a posture which might be admirable in Scottish dancing would appear ridiculous in gymnastics. It is debatable whether, from an aesthetic point of view, dance and gymnastics should ever be mixed. Perhaps the mixture was more successful with Medau gymnastics where dance-like movement predominates, than with women's Olympic gymnastics where daring and beautiful acrobatic activities are combined, on the one hand, with rigid starting and stopping positions and, on the other, with minute dance sequences which appear to lack a context. Tastes will vary; but it is surely true to say that the more stylised a system of movement becomes the more dangerous it is to mix it with any other.

Movement in Groups

The aesthetic power of even the very simplest forms of movement may be enhanced when these are performed in groups, and particularly groups in which there is some element of order. The random jostlings of a crowd may exercise a sort of hypnotic attraction and may sometimes by happy chance (or by design in a stage or film crowd scene) assume an attractive form. But this is less likely to arouse conscious admiration than the sight of persons all moving in order, like closely packed racing cyclists, cross-country runners streaming over a fence or cricketers reacting to a central magnetism as the bowler approaches the crease.

The particular attractiveness of the movements of organic groups is exemplified strongly in team sports, in stage and social dancing and in children's games.

5: Fitness and Health

The idea of being in training is one which commends itself to many young men and not a few young women. Though it is concerned with the development of physical powers it is founded essentially upon an attitude of mind—upon an appreciation of the satisfactions associated with a high level of performance and a willingness to accept a discipline in order to attain the desired level of fitness to perform. This is exactly the same whether the performer be a long distance runner, a racing driver or a concert pianist.

Regard for fitness does not always involve going into training. Indeed it could be argued that being in training is not an ideal state of affairs since it is essentially a temporary state, dependent upon the imminence of some test or challenge. When this is out of the way the discipline will be relaxed. To be in training implies the possibility, in fact the likelihood, of going out of training: and while this method of procedure may be justified in the pursuit of the kind of excellence which can only be achieved on a special occasion, the results of going out of training can sometimes be spectacularly unfortunate. It may be thought better if the training idea can be backed up by a regard for fitness which has a more permanent character; which can, in fact, be considered as an abiding personal characteristic of the individual concerned. It is certainly attractive to physical educationists to believe that fitness has a self-evident, intrinsic and permanent value; but this is an idea which, on examination, may not prove to be completely acceptable.

Most people would condemn the total disregard of physical condition which is a corollary of sloth and self-indulgence. This is generally felt to be repugnant on aesthetic if not on moral grounds; but this general repugnance is certainly not enough to justify the devotion of time and energy to an active pursuit of fitness at any high level. It may be of interest to examine some of the attitudes of mind which can on occasion lead to such a pursuit.

At one extreme is the timidity of the valetudinarian who keeps in good physical condition purely as a form of 'looking after himself'. He adopts a regime of diet and exercise which carefully avoids the possibility of harm or danger. He is not usually interested in competitive sport—though he may keep records of his performance indices, along with his weight, heart rate and blood pressure, and he becomes upset if these begin to go wrong. He is fearful of injury.

At an opposite extreme is the Spartan who follows a hard punishing programme with the aim of toughening his body and his spirit by the endurance of self-imposed stresses and privations. He undertakes hard and prolonged exercise as part of this regime. He is ready to risk injury, pneumonia and even ridicule. Value in any particular achievement is not his main concern. For him fitness justifies itself as the ability to endure.

In both these examples the stricture of Lawrence would apply: 'To have your own physique on your mind . . . is a semi-pathological state, the exact counterpoise to the querulous, peevish invalid'.

Yet another extreme type is the man who has come to possess an appetite for exercise—a positive enjoyment of large amounts of physical activity. This, in itself, is amiable enough unless it becomes linked with an excessive interest in food, drink and sleep, when it can rightly be considered a form of self indulgence. Plato[1] complains of the bodily habit of the athletes he sees about him: 'It is a drowsy condition. They sleep their life away.'

A consideration of these cases, extreme though they are, is sufficient to suggest dangers in the concept of fitness for its own sake. For the physical educationist who believes that a lasting concern for physical fitness should be one of the main outcomes of his teaching there appear to be two safeguards. One lies in the classic advocacy of moderation and a balanced view of things. Matthew Arnold[2] quotes Epictetus with approval: 'It is the sign of a nature not finely tempered to give yourselves up to things that relate to the body: to make a great fuss about exercise, a great fuss about eating, a great fuss about drinking, a great fuss about walking, a great fuss about riding. All these things ought to be done merely by the way: the formation of the spirit and the character must be our first concern'.

---

[1]Plato, *Republic*, Book III, 403.
[2]Matthew Arnold, *Culture and Anarchy*, Murray, 1924, p.14.

The other safeguard is to return to the idea of training. This is what Lawrence would have us do: 'If you will have the gymnasium: and certainly let us have the gymnasium: let it be to get us ready for the great contests and games of skill . . . Let all physical culture be pure *training*: training for the contest and training for the expressive dance'.[1] The physical educationist will almost certainly wish to have a wider range of objectives than this, and he may well wish to inclued the idea of more general preparedness to meet the varied unforeseen challenges of an active life. Physical enterprise, the habit of activity and the desire to be fit are developed alongside each other. The distinction between ends and means may, with advantage, become blurred and there may be justifiable satisfaction in the experience and proof of fitness. But there should be no doubt that fitness and training are there to promote achievement and the real value must lie in the achievement.

Fitness can be thought of as a state of functional preparedness, largely physiological in character and therefore relatively stable— unlike 'form', which has a strong psychological element and may be lost suddenly and unaccountably. For certain kinds of highly competitive activity, the concept of fitness is sometimes stretched to include a psychological element but this is not what physical fitness is usually taken as meaning. Unlike psychological fitness, or intellectual fitness or moral fitness which are always qualified by reference to what the fitness is for, physical fitness and medical fitness are often referred to in quite a general way. We say a man is physically fit or medically fit and leave it at that. This can only be because physical fitness and medical fitness are conventionally seen in relation to a much more readily understood range of tests, activities and experiences than are other forms of fitness. Medical fitness or 'a clean bill of health' means that a person is not suffering from, or noticeably sickening for, any identifiable ailment or disease. Physical fitness, more positive than this, means that a person has achieved an acceptably high level of his potential for doing physical work. It is important to realise that the standard achieved is always seen in relation to the performer's supposed potential. The concept of fitness is not related to absolute external standards but to the achievement

---

[1] D. H. Lawrence, *Phoenix*, 1936, p.652.

of the highest standards of which the individual is capable. A small ectomorphic person may be considered magnificently fit though in absolute terms his strength levels are not high. He is 'as fit as a flea'. Four hundred metres in fifty seconds may indicate a lack of fitness in one athlete and the peak of fitness in another. We look at an athlete, or a paraplegic or an old man and we assess their fitness by very different standards.

Although fitness is difficult or impossible to measure, it is, as a concept, quite firmly established. Part of its character is that it reflects the efforts of a person to attain it. We say of an athlete, or a paraplegic, or an old man: 'He keeps himself very fit'. This he does by (a) the avoidance of harmful habits and indulgences and (b) exercise and practice. The term practice (as distinct from exercise) indicates that, particularly with athletes and other specialist performers (such as musicians or dancers), the active part of training may take the same form as the finished performance. Though the high jumper, the ballerina or the pianist may, at times, go through routines aimed at general muscular or cardio-vascular effect—physical exercises or long walks—for the most part they engage in practice—of jumps, steps or scales—where no attempt is made to distinguish between fitness and skill. It almost seems as though fitness as a separate concept has disappeared. This state of affairs is reflected (conversely) in the attitude of much less serious performers who sometimes say that they play a game 'in order to keep fit.' But here the distinction is implicit. Fitness is something related to, but distinct from, ability at this or that particular activity.

For many people, the criterion of fitness is not one of ability or performance levels but rather of how they *feel* during and after a period of activity. The person who says 'I feel fit' usually assumes that this pronouncement has significance without further verification. If he feels fit he is fit: that is what fitness is all about. Even at serious competitive levels where fitness is evaluated in objective terms it is not normally expected that an individual or a team can be fit without feeling fit. The feeling of well-being seems to be part of the experience.

If fitness is, in fact, partly a feeling, the concept appears to be drawing closer to that of health.

Fitness and Health

The view of medical fitness as 'a clean bill of health' incorporates the convenient and reassuring notion that if you have no ailment you are completely healthy. But this is not the way people really think and talk about health. The doctor and his patient both distinguish between poor health, fair health, good health and excellent health and, as they rise in the scale, the criteria they employ are not so much ailments as positive factors like strength, energy, appetite, resistance to fatigue and other characteristics which indicate an active interest in life. Some of these are the same factors by which we assess fitness.

Health is certainly a much more extensive concept than fitness. Health is a state of physical well-being and competence in relation to the whole demands made upon an individual as a living organism. Good health will show in the functional efficiency of the organic systems, in mental and emotional stability, in freedom from pain and in length of life. Fitness is also a state of physical well being and competence; but only in relation to the demands made upon an individual as a machine for doing physical work. Living is more than doing physical work, but in so far as the latter function figures in the former (and it will figure to some extent for all people) fitness is part of health.

Viewed as a part of health, fitness would appear to be rather vulnerable. Fitness is immediately affected by a decline in organic health. This is true whether fitness is thought of in terms of performance levels or the feeling of well-being in exercise. Examples can be quoted of athletes who have succeeded in spite of illness but it is hardly to be imagined that any person, athlete or non-athlete, could feel better or perform better for a decline in organic health. The reverse is the common experience. Also, experience seems to show that a high level of fitness is no protection against the common ailments such as colds, infectious diseases or digestive disorders.

There is an ongoing debate concerning the possible values of physical activity in relation to certain fundamental ailments such as heart disease, obesity, mental illness or the painful conditions associated with involuntary muscular tension. There is no striking measure of agreement among researchers but the general tenor of the evidence and rational supposition is favourable. Further research and development of opinion may cause interesting changes in physical education's concern in these matters. For instance the conviction may grow that in teaching muscular relaxation as an element in posture and an element in skill (together with the mental relaxation that is associated with enjoyable recreation) physical education may benefit health even more directly than through its more usually accepted developmental functions.

A contrary factor of some importance is that vigorous physical activity contains certain dangers to health. Some measure of risk must be accepted as inherent in the nature of many of the activities (physical risk may be justifiably accepted by a mature performer as part of the attraction of a sport) but there are dangers which are obscured by ignorance or wrong attitudes and these it is the clear duty of the physical educationist to correct. Prominent among these is the danger of strain on joint structures such as that likely to be caused by a sudden severe load upon the lumbar spine or a violent lateral thrust upon the knee. Medical scientists have for some time been investigating the suggestion that osteo-arthrosis is a wear-and-tear disease to which certain kinds of athletes are prone. They are also beginning to study the effects of the drugs which more and more top class athletes are finding themselves impelled to experiment with. All these are matters which the physical educationist must keep under close review. As an educationist his priorities must never be in doubt. A calculated risk of injury is something which he may allow his pupil voluntarily to accept. A practice which will certainly endanger his pupil's health must never be condoned.

There is no simple relationship between exercise and health. Rather than pin his faith on any specific prophylactic virtues of exercise the physical educationist may prefer to maintain that habits of activity and an interest in physical fitness will go hand in hand to justify themselves in that aspect of health which is fuller living. The person who values fitness will independently safeguard his organic health. For instance, he will not smoke.

Fitness and Physical Education

The primary duty of the physical education teacher is to arouse and foster an interest in skilled physical performance. This will form a rational basis for a desire to be fit.

In the early years a child's interest is likely to be directed towards a wide variety of skills and though, in later years, the individual pupil may focus his attention on one or more particular games or activities, the teacher may well consider that a broad range of skill interests and a willingness to learn new skills is one of the hallmarks of a successful physical education. This will carry with it a concern for fitness which is general and permanent rather than specific and temporary.

An interest in fitness seems to indicate a self-consciousness and a seriousness of purpose that would be out of place in young children. The teacher of young children may be fully aware that their play and practice movements have a valuable effect in building up strength and endurance—in other words physical fitness, but it is neither necessary nor desirable that the attention of the child should be directed towards fitness or training. It is different with the adolescent. He is rightly beginning to develop an idea of himself and to identify himself with serious interests and fields of achievement in an adult world and the idea of fitness training is entirely appropriate.

Having encouraged the desire to be fit it is the duty of the teacher to explain the principles upon which fitness training is based and to devise and administer suitable fitness training programmes. He should always have in mind the value of educating pupils to the stage where they can devise effective fitness programmes for themselves.

Physiological and methodological aspects of fitness training are adequately outlined in the textbooks. Broadly speaking there are three objectives. The first is circulo-respiratory endurance or stamina. This is fundamental and universally accepted as the first criterion of fitness. It is cultivated through prolonged activity, usually of a total-body nature and always prominently involving the large muscles of the legs. Typical activities are long walks, cross country running and work-outs on the track or in the gymnasium. Fartlek and interval-running are examples of the many systems of outdoor stamina training; and circuit training is an example of indoor training where the idea of continuous activity is employed for circulo-respiratory effect.

The second objective is muscular strength. For the purposes of measurement a distinction is sometimes drawn between strength and muscular endurance—strength being measured in terms of the maximum force which can be developed in a particular movement and muscular endurance in terms of the number of times the movement can be repeated without pause against a specified, fairly heavy, load. In common usage the word 'strength' covers both these measures. A man's strength is expected to enable him not only to lift a heavy weight on one occasion but to do heavy work for a period of time. Only the exercise physiologist and the weight lifting specialist would distinguish between strength and muscular endurance as training objectives. The exact nature of the training is certain to be influenced by the nature of the task for which the training is a preparation but in general it can be said that strength is cultivated through activities in which either the whole body or a particular part of the body works against a larger than normal load. Unlike stamina which is a central function of the bodily system, strength varies between one part of the body and another. A person with weak legs may have a strong grip. Therefore strength training must be carefully organised on anatomical lines. It is generally recognised that increase in strength depends upon the application of the principle of 'overload', which postulates that training must continuously increase not so much in the amount as in the intensity—peak load—of the work done. Though strength can be developed through callisthenic exercises and through such activities as rope climbing and bar work, it is in weight training that the 'overload' principle can be most accurately and conveniently applied and this is why weights are so commonly used for the quick restoration of muscle function after injury.

A high level of strength is a quality not conspicuously necessary nowadays. It is a quality in which one person will differ naturally very much from another. The small light-muscled person will never excel in feats of strength and should not be encouraged to have ambitions in that direction. But it is reasonable to believe that, under modern sedentary conditions of living, most people, even young people, are 'under strength' particularly in the upper body; easily tired and unnecessarily limited in their capacity for skilled performance in actions of a lifting, climbing or throwing nature. Any person who is interested enough to undertake fitness training is likely to see the value of increasing, or at least maintaining, the strength of the muscles of his arms, shoulders, back and abdomen. He can only do this by exercising them against loads greater than those he commonly meets in everyday life.

The third common objective of fitness training is range of joint mobility. Here, as in strength, persons will differ naturally between one and another. There are certainly no agreed norms to which one can aspire, but one has only to suffer a period of enforced fixation in a particular joint or group of joints to realise that mobility decreases at a rate and, in the end, to a completeness which is more spectacular even than the atrophy of the surrounding muscles. The effect of joint stiffness on skilled performance or graceful movement is devastating. Here again it is likely that in everyday life we never attempt to use anything like the full range of joint movement available to us. Fitness training can attempt to rectify this. Earlier methods involved the forcible stretching of muscles around a joint; modern methods depend more upon the encouragement of relaxation in the practice of active free-ranging movement. In this area of activity fitness comes close to skill.

In all this discussion fitness has been seen as closely related to participation. Many will feel that sufficient fitness can come through participation, if participation is frequent and regular. The American use of the word 'practice' rather than 'training' emphasises this idea. It has been suggested that schoolboys and schoolgirls—and indeed men and women—should want to be fit. Whether or not they should take part in specific training periods, like an athlete or a race-horse, will be a matter of opinion. Where they do, these should surely be on a voluntary basis and undertaken in moderation. What constitutes moderation will also be a matter of opinion. Moderation may be too vague an idea for a child or a young person to take as a guide to his conduct but civilised parents and teachers may, in practice, not find it too difficult to interpret. It will be their concern to ensure that a preoccupation with training and fitness does not take up too much of a young person's time and attention when other demands are taken into evaluative account.

The final justification for the idea of fitness probably lies in the cultivation of habits of activity. It is known that activity brings arousal; the mere fact of activity sharpens the senses. The ideal is surely the kind of activity and the kind of arousal which is mental as well as physical. Fitness should add zest to living.

6: Mind and Character

Mind and character have been bracketed together to represent an area of concern in physical education. They are clearly related. Mind might be said to include character: though mind is more generally associated with intellectual activity and character with habits and attitudes. Mind and character express themselves in action but their essential medium is thought. In this they differ from physical education's other areas of concern.

Intellectual and Physical Activity
It has commonly been supposed, through centuries, that participation in certain forms of athletic activity may influence character. Sometimes attempts are made to indicate conditions under which an intellectual influence may also be exerted.[1] The matter deserves careful attention. There can be no doubt that physical education involves the operation of intelligence and thought. How important a place does this give us in the field of intellectual education?

It is perhaps necessary at this point, to emphasise that what is under consideration as physical education is the actual participation in athletic activity, or the actual process of physical education, not the study of the subject, say by administrators or teachers. This latter, like the study of anything else, is primarily an intellectual exercise.

It must be assumed that a child's earliest skills are not intellectualised; that the near-random movement experiences of infants involve no separation of conscious thought from the world of raw perception and feeling. Yet out of these the mind of the child develops. Movement is involved in the whole of his learning. It is difficult to assess from the evidence[2], either experimental or anecdotal, whether move-

[1]For a review see A. D. Munrow, *Physical Education: a Discussion of Principles*, 1972, Ch.4.
[2]For a review see D. R. Morris & H. T. A. Whiting, *Motor Impairment and Compensatory Education*, 1971, Ch.3.

ment itself is a major contributory or whether movement figures incidentally as the corollary of sensory experience. And though there is ample evidence that motor and sensory deprivation will have a retarding effect upon a young child's development (presumably both mental and physical since mental development can only be guessed at in terms of motor skills) there does not seem to be any similarly conclusive evidence that a degree of activity or stimulation higher than is normal in this post-Montessorian age will benefit development. Physical activity appears to be like nutrition: it is beneficial up to a point but beyond this it has no additional value.

As the child grows older the distinctive power of the intellect will make itself apparent. Forms of activity will be undertaken in which the effects of rational thought will be distinguishable from those of physical skill. Some forms of activity—such as speech, calligraphy and a great deal of manipulation—will justify themselves primarily as embodiments of rational thought and, from this time onwards, what Ryle[1] calls 'the primacy of the intellect' will make itself felt. All actions will be, in some measure or other, in subservience to the intellect and the will. Much education will be effected through the conscious activation of the intellectual powers—through comprehension and value judgement. Much will be effected through other means—through the semi-automatic formation of habits, tastes and attitudes and through the acquisition of skills. The rational and the sensual go hand in hand. Even at a mature stage, when values are thoughtfully examined before acceptance, they may be seen to depend upon competences which can only be acquired through the world of the senses rather than that of the intellect. The point at issue is where, in this scheme of things, physical education belongs.

In so far as we are concerned with the acquisition of skills it seems we are operating at something below the level of mental involvement which would merit the term intellectual. Fundamentally we might agree with Peters:[2] 'There is little to know about riding bicycles, swimming or playing golf'. (He presumably means there is little worth knowing.) Thought and intelligence will certainly be demanded of the learner. He must 'pay attention'. He must memorise his impressions in relation to both what he sees he has achieved and

[1]Gilbert Ryle, *Concept of Mind*, 1949, p.314.
[2]R. S. Peters, *Education as Initiation*, 1963, p.30.

what he wants to achieve; otherwise he will get no value from his practice. He must constantly size up changes in the environment; otherwise he cannot adapt. All this demands mental concentration on the phenomena of the task, but not intellectual analysis or abstract thought. Certainly a skilled action can be made the subject of intellectual study but this is another process which rarely seems to justify itself as part of skill learning. A novice would surely be distracted by the theory of catching, or jumping or riding a bicycle. He is mentally alert but he is not reasoning; he is interpreting sensations; he is apprehending with nerve and muscle.

But it will be argued that physical education is more than the learning of physical skills. Learned skills must be used in highly organised forms of behaviour, often specifically designed to demand understanding as well as skill. Thus it comes about that, quite frequently, the experienced or the 'clever' performer will outshine one who possesses more physical ability. At the more advanced levels there is often the demand not only for a grasp of general principles concerning skill and tactics but for the comprehension of matters beyond the physical activity itself—such as the intricacies of an orienteering chart, the tensile strength of a nylon rope or the effect of a heavy roller.

So long as the pure activity values are firmly established (and these are the essential ones in physical education) there seems to be no reason why a performer who sees a connexion between his skill and some field of useful intellectual exercise or knowledge should not be encouraged to pursue it. The educational theorist is apt to be scornful of such exercise as merely incidental. The practising teacher takes what opportunities he comes across. A spread of interest between athletics and the mechanics of non-rigid bodies; between dance and the other arts; between caving and the earth sciences; between skill and fitness; these may all be growing points in the education of a boy or girl. The operative words are 'may be'. A warning against exaggerating the importance of physical activity is contained in a reminiscence of Violet Bonham Carter.[1] When asked, as an old lady, what single factor in her childhood had contributed most to her personal development she said it was a year

---

[1]Kenneth Harris interview, BBC 1, 13 April, 1967.

during which she was almost totally paralysed and confined to bed. Her father was then Home Secretary. Invariably his distinguished visitors after talking to him, were conducted upstairs to talk to the small child.

The opinions of teachers and parents on this matter are varied and are probably based as much on personal taste as on observation. Some see regular vigorous physical activity as an aid to mental concentration; others see it as a distraction and even as a waste of energy. It seems true to say that in so far as it is possible to distinguish between physical and intellectual activity (and it is not possible with very young children), there is no demonstrable relationship between them. As with fitness training, the best guide appears to be common sense, sympathy and a distrust of going to extremes. Physical education will be conducted in an atmosphere which is thoughtful and open minded. There will be occasions within physical education for the acquisition of knowledge and the exercise of judgement but these do not seem to have either the predictability or the range sufficient to establish intellectual development as a major objective or function for the subject.

Integration between subjects is a fashionable idea these days. The physical educator, as an educator, cannot fail to be interested in the intellectual development and the wide cultural advancement of his pupils. He can serve this end by presenting physical education in such a way that its values are seen, strongly and unpretentiously, as balanced by, occasionally similar to, and always compatible with the values of other subjects. The teacher himself, by his conversation and his attitudes should demonstrate his interest in these other subjects. He may teach other subjects. Formal integration may, at times, present itself as a convenient and natural procedure. But it is not essential. It is in the mind of the pupil, not on the timetable, that integration must take place.

Character

Any pronouncement about character must, to some extent, reflect personal taste and opinion. Conviction can only come from an interpretation of personal experience. There is some room for difference of opinion. The following observations are made by one whose temperament and training have disposed him towards a love of athletic activity and a sympathy with those of a like mind.

From very early times the idea has been widely held that participation in certain forms of demanding physical activity, more particularly competitive athletic contests, may foster desirable traits of
character. Acceptance of the idea was more general formerly than
now. Nowadays it is fashionable to be critical, even cynical, on this
matter. The mystique attaching to traditional values (playing fields
and Waterloo) has been supplanted by a mystique attaching to
'research'. Personality is assessed in 'scientific' terms and, where it
proves impossible—as it generally does—to establish any statistical
relationship between participation in certain forms of activity and
the formation of particular character traits, there is a tendency to
believe that such a relationship does not exist. Not only is the lack of
experimental evidence, one way or another, used to support an
iconoclastic attitude but what anecdotal evidence there is is generally used to the same effect. A cricketer who is a good sport in everyday life is held to prove nothing: a cricketer who is a bad sport is
held to demolish the whole idea of sportsmanship.

Perhaps earlier enthusiasts were too general in their claims.
Froebel[1] wrote: 'I also studied the boys' play, the whole series of
games in the open air, and learned to recognise their mighty power
to awake and to strengthen the intelligence and the soul as well as
the body. In these games and what was connected with them I
detected the mainspring of the moral strength which animated the
pupils and young people in the institution. The games, as I am now
fervently assured, formed a mental bath of extraordinary strengthen-
ing power and although the sense of the higher symbolic meaning
of games had not yet dawned on me, I was nevertheless able to
perceive, in each boy genuinely at play, a moral strength governing
both mind and body which won my highest esteem.' Since Froebel,
Durkheim has written a major treatise on Moral Education without
once mentioning games and in much of the current writing games
are only mentioned in order to label them as unimportant.[2] It is
clear that any attempt made nowadays to defend even a little of the
old position must be made in very deliberate terms.

Peters has examined the use of the word character and from among
several distinct meanings he puts forward two which are of particular
significance in the present discussion. There is the individual char-

---

[1] F. W. A. Froebel, *Autobiography*, Trans. Michaelis & Moore, Allen, 1915, p.82.
[2] Cf. Deardon, quoted p.16.

acter, good, bad or indifferent, which everyone has. This is an amal-
gam of personal traits. Then there is character in the abstract,
which not everyone has. Not everyone is a man or woman of
character—a man or woman whose conduct is governed by moral
principle.[1]

Moral Education
Peters' distinction seems to coincide with a distinction which emerges
from almost all the writing on moral education—a distinction between two forms or two stages in the process. There is the form, or
the stage, of moral education which attempts to mould the immature
person. He is led to form habits of thought and action, to cultivate
sensitivities and accept values which carry adult approval. Beyond
this is the stage at which he is encouraged to regulate his conduct
for himself through understanding and rational thought.

The second stage is, of course, logically superior. It might be held
to supersede the first, though experience seems to show that habits
and attitudes—good or bad—acquired during the suggestible period
of childhood have a lasting quality which subsequent understanding
and rationality find it hard to erase. It should clearly be the aim of
any scheme of moral education to inculcate habits and attitudes in
the early stages which are likely to earn the approval, rather than
the disapproval, of the pupil when he reaches the stage of critical
autonomous judgement.

It might be questioned whether the two stages are as distinct as at
first appears. Even Durkheim[2] who entirely approves of the mould-
ing element in moral education points out the dangers of allotting
a too passive role to the child. He suggests that at every stage the
child's initiative should be stimulated as well as his compliance
sought. Automatic responses, whether of thought or action will
stand in need, even at an early stage, of some reinforcement from
the building up of simple moral concepts.

Perhaps the issue will be clarified by reference once again to
Peters.[3] He suggests that the methods by which moral education (or
character development) may be effected are threefold: example,

[1]R. S. Peters, *Authority and Responsibility in Education*, 1963, Ch.9.
[2]Emile Durkheim, *Moral Education*, Free Press, 1961, p.153.
[3]R. S. Peters, *op. cit.* p.117.

rational discussion and practical experience. At the earliest stages rational discussion will be limited. Difficult aspects of moral problems may even be deliberately concealed. The child will learn by observing the conduct of his elders and by constant practice himself. But the kind of situation in which his practice is likely to have a truly moral effect is a situation in which he can recognise a degree of universality. He must be kind not only to his pet dog, he must be kind to animals. He must not only not be afraid of the dark, but he must be brave.

The need to use situations with a general relevance has sometimes led to a criticism of play activities as the stuff of moral education. We are told that play is divided off from real life. Moral issues must be real issues. Decisions must be taken and acts performed which are seen to be part of the reality of life not the make-believe of games. To one who can remember the intensity and the seriousness of a boy's involvement in a game—the importance of performing creditably oneself (both as to skill and conduct) and the thrill of a good game unmarred by deficiency or default—to such a person the distinction between reality and play seems rather academic. To sacrifice 'real' things, such as one's lunch, or spend a week's pocket money, rather than miss a chance of playing in an attractive match, would be to sacrifice things comparatively unimportant.

Of course not all boys or girls feel this degree of involvement but for those who do it seems reasonable to believe that competitive games provide a field of activity where the interest and the striving are real, where the difference between good and not so good, even between right and wrong, are sufficiently clear to serve as material for practice in behaviour. To believe that a moral lesson is useless except in precisely the circumstances in which it was learned is to deny the possibility of moral education. There seems to be no conceivable reason why a child should not apprehend moral concepts of a general value—and cement them by practice—during his involvement in games. The guidance must be there, the personal contact, the example and, occasionally, the precept, but, if these are provided, the other requisite, the opportunity for constant practice under testing conditions, is there in good measure.

All this is no more than stating a conviction, based on rational thought, that games can, under certain circumstances, serve as useful experience in moral education or character training. Whether they do commonly serve this purpose, in any significant measure, is a different question. And there are other questions too. Are games and competitive athletics more suited for the development of certain characteristics than others? What is the likelihood that, under the wrong conditions, bad characteristics rather than good may be the outcome? Do the other main constituents of physical education, such as outdoor activities and dance, operate in the same way as competitive athletics and games?

These are questions to which researchers and teachers should continue to give their attention. Teachers cannot wait for the results of the research. They must act. But they must also think. They must study the problems in the light of their experience in a search for rational convictions. In the absence of explicit data it is likely that such convictions will be of a liberal rather than a restrictive nature. Things will be tried out. In no other aspect of physical education is the dictum of Plato more apposite: 'The best training is simple and flexible'.[1] It is in complication and rigidity of ideas that error is likely to lie. Meanwhile there are certain pieces of research into the personality of athletes which seem to throw some light on the problems under discussion.[2]

Two of the better known personality theories are indicated in the diagram which follows. Eysenck (1965) postulated two dimensions, (1) extroversion-introversion and (2) neuroticism (emotionality). These are represented by the continuous lines. Claridge (1967) suggested that Eysenck's two dimensions might both contribute to a third dimension based on arousal, a term indicating a state in which the whole nervous system is alerted and sensitised towards the receipt of stimuli. Athletes are shown, by and large, to be extrovert and low in neuroticism; this places them low on the arousability scale. There are many exceptions to this general rule. Women athletes, while extrovert like the men, show rather higher emotionality. There is some research to indicate, as one would expect, differences between participants in different sports. But the overall picture of athletes is that they are extrovert and emotionally stable.

---

[1]Plato, *Republic*, Book III, 403.
[2]For a review, see J. E. Kane, *Psychological Aspects of Sport and Physical Education*, 1972, Ch.4.

They are likely to exhibit characteristics which fall into two categories. In the first category are toughmindedness, high confidence, low anxiety, adventurousness and tolerance of pain: these tend to produce behaviour marked by physical courage. In the second category are hunger for stimulus and human company, cheerfulness, mental relaxation and lack of psychological 'drive'; these amount to a disposition towards sociability.

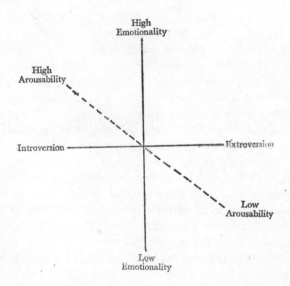

No causal relationship has been established between athletic participation and the development of characteristics such as these, but the only research of which there is any record concerns short-term experiments upon adults. It is more prolonged exposure particularly with young children that one would expect to have an effect upon character. It can be assumed that persons of an extrovert temperament will be attracted towards competitive games in the first place and will persist with them when less sympathetically inclined persons would give them up. And it seems reasonable to suppose that the extrovert tendencies of such persons will be reinforced by participation. It is a small step from this to believe that extrovert tendencies that were at first entirely latent might, through athletics or other similar experience, become established as overt characteristics. What does seem in line both with the findings of the personality researchers and the comments of observers through the centuries is that any changes in attitude or changes in behaviour stemming from participation in athletics are likely to be in the direction of extroversion—that is toughness, cheerfulness and sociability —and not in the opposite direction of wide sensitivity or intensity of feeling. Russell[1] takes a frankly behavioural view of morality, at any rate where young children are concerned. He firmly believes that physical courage can be developed through training. 'A man is courageous when he does things which others might fail to do owing to fear. If he feels no fear so much the better. . . . The secret of modern moral education is to produce results by means of good habits which were formerly produced (or attempted) by self control and will power'. Furthermore he saw a connexion between courage and skill. He wrote: 'It is a valuable experience which stimulates both self respect and effort to pass gradually from fear to skill. Even so simple a matter as learning to ride a bicycle will give this experience in a mild form' and though he expresses a preference for adventurous outdoor pursuits rather than games and contests he does not press this preference too far. 'I should train school children in forms of more or less dangerous dexterity rather than in such things as football . . . I do not mean that this principle should be applied pedantically, but that it should be allowed more weight in athletics than is the case at present.'

Aggression and Sportsmanship
If we believe that extrovert tendencies can be reinforced with good effect through a particular form of training we must surely admit that the process can be carried to excess. Aggressive behaviour is part and parcel of many sports and it tends to appear in all forms of competition. Whatever view is taken of the biological significance of aggression it is clearly something that the games master must keep under control. Lorenz[2] believes that aggression is natural and inevitable; it is dangerous if bottled up and is best worked off in the

---

[1]Bertrand Russell, *On Education*, 1926, p.92.
[2]Conrad Lorenz, *On Aggression*, 1966.

simulated hostilities of activities such as competitive sports. Other biologists take a different view:[1] some experiments with apes seem to demonstrate that aggressive behaviour is learned by the young of the species from aggressive older males. If this is true we may in fact be cultivating aggressive tendencies rather than finding an outlet for them in our games playing.

All this emphasises a point which ought to be obvious anyway. No medium is of any value in moral education which is not at the same time potentially dangerous. The situations which present opportunities for truly brave or kind acts are those which also present alternatives; not only for the direct opposites, cowardice or selfishness, but for all kinds of excesses, evasion or pretences which may be morally harmful. Much that passes for sport these days, both professional and amateur, is brutal, dishonest and utterly selfish. Many teachers may wish to keep children from all contact with it. Others may take Plato's view: 'He who, as boy and man, endures the test and issues from it unspoiled we must establish as ruler over our city'.

Sport has undoubtedly contributed ideas of moral import to our national outlook and our language—ideas contained in expressions such as 'It's all part of the game', 'Fair play' and 'Sportsmanship'. The fact that these phrases are now used more widely outside sport than within, completely demonstrates what is sometimes denied by the pundits, that concepts born in sport can have a general relevance. The first expression represents a light-heartedness in the face of mischance which, when taken together with a real interest in the game and a real desire to win, is surely an aid to sanity, realism and civilised behaviour. Fair play embodies an important moral concept which transcends the rules of the game. To say 'It's not fair' is to make an absolute moral judgement not based on any study of man-made rules or laws. A child may say it's not fair that small Chinese should play against tall Americans at basketball. When told the rules allow it he says 'It's still not fair'. The concept of natural justice will, of course, be brought home to the child in his non-play activities but to have it enshrined in a play phrase gives it point and prominence. Sportsmanship goes one degree further. It means being a little more generous to an opponent than the rules of the game or

[1]See for instance D. Hamburg, 'Recent Research on Aggressive Behaviour,' Vickers Lecture, 1970, Mental Health Research Fund: London.

even the idea of fair play demands; but only a *little* more generous—not in any demonstrative way and certainly not in any way that will imply patronage or take the keen edge off the competition. One's colleagues must be considered as well as one's opponents. Sportsmanship is more often expressed by a refusal to take a fortuitous advantage oneself than by attempting to confer one on one's opponent. It is therefore quite a sophisticated idea, calling for the exercise of delicacy, tact and understanding of the competitive situation.

Competition

Competition is an element in behaviour which merits some attention from theorists in physical education since it figures more prominently in our activities than in those of other subjects. This is often held to our disadvantage, the argument being that competition is unnecessarily stressful and that competitiveness, as a personal characteristic, is unattractive.

Competition involves the pitting of one person or one team against another team. It is distinct from other forms of endeavour. A man who is striving against the difficulties of a rock face or against the elements is not engaged in competition (except that in a figurative sense he may attribute a personality to the difficulties that face him; and this is a dangerous error). No questions of inter-personal rivalry arise. But even when the concept of competition has been clarified by excluding everything but inter-personal rivalry it still includes two fundamentally different forms of behaviour. The simplest is taking part in an activity which is *by nature* competitive, like playing football or running in a race. The other arises from finding oneself in a position of rivalry in some sphere of activity which is not *by nature* competitive; it may involve running a shop next door to a similar existing shop or applying, along with other people, for a particular job. Entering a music competition belongs to this category. Competition is a *necessary* part of football; it is not a *necessary* part of shopkeeping, or finding suitable employment or playing a sonata. It just happens that some of the good things of life are in limited supply and people must compete for them. It is this second, and more general, form of competition which is stressful to all concerned, winners and losers. Most people, while accepting it, do not enjoy it. But there are some who do. These are the really competitive people, activated not by a desire to do well and earn acclaim, or even to obtain the good things of life, but by a positive enjoyment of beating the others. This is an unattractive characteristic and there are absolutely no grounds for believing that the typical extrovert games player—relaxed, cheerful, unemotional, rather insensitive and not easily roused—is a particularly competitive sort of person in this wider sense.

The competitive element in games and athletics is acceptable because it is inbuilt and therefore limited. It can hardly be thought —even in our boyish Anglo-Saxon culture—that competitive games are important as a means of demonstrating superiority. They are not particularly reliable as tests anyway. The phrase 'may the best man win' indicates clearly that this outcome is not expected automatically. Footballers do not choose football because it is competitive but because it is football. The competition happens to be part of football and anyone who does not enjoy the total experience—competition and all—will not choose to play. The particular game justifies itself as an occasion. The better team may not win and this adds to the interest.

The degree of concern with winning or losing must fit the occasion. In an affair on the front lawn nobody is expected to try too hard. Sometimes (say in tennis or basketball) opponents will compete for individual points, one after another, without bothering to keep the score. On the other hand, in a representative match it is a concern with the final result which gives point to the game.

It is always possible that the issue may be allowed to assume an importance which embitters the occasion. The remedy for us as educators would appear to be twofold. Firstly we must cultivate the idea among all competitors of an immediate 'switching off' of tension the moment the final whistle goes. This must be absolute. Secondly we must do everything possible to make the game in its setting, its preliminaries and, very particularly, its subsequences, a completely attractive occasion. Not every race can end as did Wordsworth's boat race on 'an island musical with birds' but we can aim to make the pleasures of the occasion so outweigh the concern with defeat or victory that we may approach his state of mind:

'*In such a race*
So ended, disappointment could be none,
Uneasiness or pain or jealousy:
We rested in the shade, all pleased alike,
Conquered and conqueror. Thus the pride of strength
And the vain-glory of superior skill,
Were tempered: Thus was gradually produced
A quiet independence of the heart'.[1]

Non-competitive Activities

The foregoing discussion concerning physical education and its relation to character has centred almost entirely on competitive games and athletics. If attention is turned to other branches of physical education, notably outdoor activities and dance, certain differences would suggest themselves.

Outdoor activities are commonly compared with games as the material for character training, and often to the latter's disadvantage. Scott wrote in his last diary: 'Make the boy interested in natural history if you can: it is better than games'. Russell has already been quoted as saying the same sort of thing. The Outward Bound Trust has become a symbol of the faith many people have in the good influence of outdoor activities upon the development of character. Reasons in support of this belief are readily forthcoming. Outdoor pursuits are felt to be closer to real life and certainly closer to nature than are games. The operations are more various and the problems more compelling. Survival is sometimes at stake. Adventure arises not only from the element of physical danger but from the constant opportunities for travel and new experience.

Perhaps it may be felt that games and outdoor adventure have complementary values based on an essential difference. There is more fun and laughter in games. Games are essentially sociable; they flourish in a gregarious atmosphere. Outdoor pursuits, while stressing, even more than games, the need for co-operative effort among small groups, seem to demand, as their ultimate stage, an escape from society.

Dance is different again. It is not generally put forward as having

---

[1]Wordsworth, *The Prelude*, Book II, pp.65-72.

any particular function where character development is concerned. Nevertheless, it must be assumed that a powerful interest in dance, like any other powerful interest, is capable of exercising an influence upon the development of mental and emotional attitudes.

Dance is neither competitive nor adventurous. In its simpler manifestations it is an enjoyable social activity. At a more sophisticated level it becomes a rather free art form, more 'make believe' even than games since it exists by the creation of an illusion. Like other art forms it is sometimes credited with the power of freeing the spirit, especially through the removal of inhibitions among persons who are unable or reluctant to express themselves. As with outdoor activities and games it seems justifiable to suspect that those who habitually practise the activity are those who find it congenial, that is those who already possess the personal qualities which the activity seems likely to develop. Therefore, just as the teacher of competitive activities must guard against the over-development of aggressive characteristics, so must the teacher of dance guard against exhibitionism and the over-cultivation of sensitivity. One benefit that may arise out of the incorporation of dance within physical education is that the dancer may be encouraged to think of himself as an athlete —a special sort of athlete but an athlete none the less.

The Character of the School

It is perhaps not too fanciful to conclude a section on character by reflecting that character is a quality not only of individuals but of institutions and societies.

Societies and the individuals that compose them are continually reacting on one another. As educators we may frequently feel that the best way to influence the characters of individual boys and girls is by improving the character of the community in which they move.

'All work and no play makes Jack a dull boy' and it might be thought to make the school a dull place too. In no other school subject are work and play so well mixed as in physical education. The acquisition of the necessary skills involves assiduous practice and application. Fitness involves bodily fatigue and discomfort. The decision to take part often involves a willingness to accept a challenge and the possible disappointment of failure. These are all hard things to endure and hard to learn, like so much else that has to be learnt in school. They will not be learnt unless the essential attractiveness of the physical education programme is felt and acknowledged. When things conspire to produce a good physical education programme this will surely contribute not only an element of variety and lightheartedness but of respect for physical skill and physical beauty which will uplift the character of the school.

7: Values

The term 'physical education' itself constitutes a claim that education can be effected through certain well known forms of physical activity.

Though these forms of physical activity are disparate they have certain characteristics in common: they all employ free, vigorous, skilful total body movements and find their value and justification within the activities themselves.

Such a collection of characteristics might be thought sufficient to mark these movements as athletic in nature (whatever else they are). The actions of a brewer's drayman might be called athletic provided attention is fixed on the power, fluency and zest of the performer rather than on the number of barrels he moves from one place to another. On the other hand the action of a robot or a galley slave would not be called athletic. The term implies intention and feeling as well as form.

It is unfortunate for the present purpose, that the terms 'athlete' and 'athletics' have acquired more restricted meanings. We think of an athlete and a dancer as being different and distinct. Yet the movements of a dancer are, in the truest sense, athletic. They are free, skilful, total-body movements and just as obviously as those of the competitive athlete, are performed for values found in the movements themselves. The degree of vigour demanded will vary from time to time and from one dance form to another, but, in general, dance is characterised by a much higher level of vigorous involvement than that of everyday life. Among modern professional performers there is an unmistakable interest in physical stamina and physical power. Modern dancers often give performances in athletic clothing and—unlike many physical educationists—they even talk of 'physical training'. Similarly, in outdoor activities, many of the essential skills, such as rock climbing, ski-ing and canoeing are, by any standards, athletic.

It cannot be too strongly emphasised that this does not imply that dance and outdoor pursuits are simply athletic activities. Each has its own character and can appear in its own right inside or outside physical education. So, for that matter, can games. The point is that this athletic quality is the one quality common to all physical education activities and it is always possible that it may prove to be more than an accidental or purely descriptive link. It may indicate a common significant value. This will be examined later. At this point it needs to be said that the admission that a common value is possible, and would indeed be attractive, does not mean that such a common value is a theoretical necessity for the concept of physical education, or would overshadow all other values. Physical education can quite well be regarded as a collection of differing activities, linked by certain 'family resemblances' and considered worthwhile for a variety of reasons.[1]

To return to the first sentence of this chapter, the term, and therefore, presumably, the concept of physical education, seems to demand that the values attaching to it shall integrate with those of the larger process of total education. A physically educated person must, by definition, be an educated person. If we could imagine a person who was completely lacking in formal schooling and yet who could be considered physically educated, it would surely be that, through the means of physical contact with his environment and the influence of this contact upon his thoughts and emotions, he had acquired some measure of culture. Physical skill and physical power are not enough: these must be directed by active and rational thought, awareness of beauty and humane values. It follows that, in a modern context, although it is possible to distinguish the processes of physical education from the rest of a child's schooling (and indeed it is essential to do this if the term is to have any meaning) it is not possible completely to distinguish its values.

Education
One difficulty that the physical education theorist may feel at the moment is that a rather restrictive element has recently found its

---

[1] Cf. Molly Adams, *Concept of Physical Education II*, 'Proc. Philosophy of Educ. Soc.,' Vol. III, Jan. 1969.

way into the concept of education. Peters[1] may not have intended all that has been inferred when he postulated the importance of 'the cognitive aspect of the content of education'. He sees a cognitive content as being essential in enabling a pupil to see what he is doing in relation to other things in life—to obtain 'a perspective that is not too limited'. The perspective is not a new idea. John Dewey[2] speaks of giving a person 'the education that enables him to see in his daily work all there is in it of large and human significance'. The two men develop this idea rather differently in relation to skills. Peters[3] asserts: 'Few skills have a wide-ranging cognitive content'. It seems that the cognitive content which at first was thought of as a means to the vision is now being treated as an end or a good in its own right. This is certainly a common interpretation of Peters. For some, the cognitive content has come to dominate the idea of education. Dewey,[4] on the other hand, (who has the same perspective) justifies the introduction of skills—manual training, sewing, cooking—'not on purpose . . . but by instinct, by experimenting and finding that such work takes a vital hold on pupils and gives them something which is not to be got in any other way'. And he goes on to make favourable reference to games and sports. Peters[5] characteristically states that 'games can be conceived of as being of educational importance only insofar as they provide opportunities for acquiring knowledge, qualities of mind, character and skill that have application in a wider area of life'. Plato would have agreed with him and seen no difficulty about justifying games —the right sort of games—on these grounds. This would be the position of many physical educationists. But nowadays—without entirely rejecting this sterner view—we are more inclined to think with Ivor Brown that 'it is the function of games to diversify and decorate the business of living'. Diversification and decoration may not have much educational significance for Peters (or Plato, for that matter). One feels they would appeal to Dewey[6] who saw the school as a place for 'learning? . . . certainly; but living primarily'. There is more than one view of education.

---

[1]R. S. Peters, *Education as Initiation*, 1963, pp.26-31.
[2]John Dewey, *School and Society*, Ch. I, Phoenix, 1965, p.24.
[3]Peters.   [4]Dewey, Ch.I, p.13.
[5]Peters.   [6]Dewey, Ch.II, p.36.

Values in Physical Education

The physical educationist may feel inclined to seek justification for his activities both on the grounds of direct satisfactions and of training value. The discussions in earlier chapters of this book suggest that such an attempt may be made on the following lines.

Direct satisfactions

1) Kinetic experience
2) Mental (emotional) experience

Benefits from training

1) Social adequacy
2) Physical fitness and total health
3) Effects on character

Kinetic Experience

Is this the common value we are looking for? There does seem to be a unique satisfaction in the experience of large, free, sure and powerful movement which is important for the self-realisation of every individual. The child who has not climbed to a height, swung from one foothold to another, vaulted over obstacles, swum in deep water, caught a flying missile or responded to the rhythms of the dance, has missed significant opportunities to know himself. He may, like the paralysed child referred to earlier, have obtained full value from opportunities of another kind. He may be stimulated by the very lack of motor experience to seek experiences of another kind. But as a complete individual he will have been deprived.

Experience depends upon skill but it is important to recognise, at the outset, that the value lies in the experience and not the level of expertise. Skill is a fine thing. But in this context it must be seen by the educator as a means to experience and not as an end in itself. The nervous uncoordinated child who, after difficulty, learns to swim and to love swimming may be gaining more from swimming than the school champion.

It would be wrong to think of kinetic experience as a simple automatic sensation. It is a complex personal reaction to many different kinds of sensation—visual, tactile, auditory, proprioceptive—and it may include factors deriving from comprehension and skill. But consciousness need not go beyond the phenomena of the actual movement. It is the sort of satisfaction that an artist or a house painter might conceivably feel in an expert brush stroke; but the point of the present argument is that this kind of satisfaction is more likely in a large, free brush stroke than a small tightly controlled one. The largest and free-est movements are athletic movements.

Kinetic experience, like religious, aesthetic or any other kind of experience can only be recognised from within the person. It cannot be demonstrated. All that can be said from the point of view of public recognition is that this seems to be a fairly common sort of experience. Even persons who have never been fortunate enough to experience the satisfactions of athletic activity, but who remember the intense pleasure of moving after a long confinement in bed, will admit the possibility that to move freely and adventurously adds a dimension to living. Not everyone feels this as strongly as Lawrence.[1] To him it is a matter of being in tune 'with the omnipresent centre-pull of the earth's great gravity'. And he continues: 'Without this we are nothing: clumsy mechanical clowns'.

Of course this sort of satisfaction spills over into the satisfactions which are predominantly mental in character. (The example of the artist and the house painter makes this very clear.)

Mental satisfaction

The essential thing here is that the form in which the activity is organised should be such as will give opportunities for the play of the intelligence and the imagination. The staple items of the physical education curriculum may without difficulty be organised and presented in such a way. Since the activities are, by our definition, 'athletic', it goes without saying that the pure motor satisfactions will not be lacking, but, as any pupil will tell us, the activity must be 'interesting' if it is to hold attention for any length of time.

The mental interest, and with it the possibility of emotional involvement in the activities of the physical education programme may stem from either of two sources. There is the excitement and the humour associated with unpredictability of outcome. This is related to the problem-solving element always present in competitive play (even in puzzles and after-dinner party games) and it appears

---

[1] D. H. Lawrence, *Phoenix*, 1936, p.652.

in the pleasurable tension often associated with outdoor adventure pursuits. It thrives on such factors as surprise, incongruity, risk of failure and even a certain amount of physical danger. The English word for it is 'fun'.

Fun constitutes a major value in physical education, whether considered as a direct enrichment of the texture of life or as a compensation against stress.

Secondly there are satisfactions associated with skilled achievement. It has been pointed out several times in these pages that physical education activities are not constructive in the sense that artifacts are produced. But in the more sophisticated physical activities the child is invited not only to move and enjoy moving or to 'chance his arm' in competition or adventure for the fun of it, but to act creatively, to perform well because a good performance has value. The existence of such intrinsic value with well-understood standards is generally accepted without much question by performers and knowledgeable spectators. 'That was a good one', they say. If asked why, they may give an explanation in mechanical or quantitative terms related to the known function of the movement, but in fact the judgement is based on a contemplation of the form of the movement and so is, in some degree aesthetic. A person who could not see the performance but was only watching a quantitative recording on a radar screen—say number of inches jumped or nearness of the ball to the wicket—might still say 'That was a good one', but he would only be reporting what he took to be a fact; he would not be making a value judgement.

To say that the judgements of good and bad movements are 'to some degree aesthetic' is perhaps as near the truth as we can get. Aesthetic is a word which, in the hands of experts has a very special and very refined meaning; so it is probably better to claim no more than that our judgements of quality in football or cricket approach this 'to some degree'. This is sufficient to make the point that the judgements are usually *not* based—as some people think—purely on outcomes. They are based on form. (Form of course, includes outcome; the total form, or external aspect of an action, usually makes success or failure clear.) A footballer or a supporter in the crowd might, if given the choice, prefer a wretched fumbling miskick which happened to score a goal, to a brilliant shot countered by a brilliant save. But this would only be because, for various reasons unconnected with values in the game, and certainly unconnected with physical education (reasons associated rather with status, or money, or league points), he wanted above all things to win. He would still not call the miskick 'a good one'. He might call the good shot—or for that matter the save—'a beauty'.

There appears to be some difference here between dance and the other activities in physical education. Dancers are, it seems, consciously concerned with the beauty of their movements, athletes are not. The athlete is much closer to the craftsman than to the artist. The job of the craftsman is to produce an object which is totally good—not one which just happens, by accident, to serve its purpose or one which is acceptable because there is nothing better to hand. An object which is totally good functions well and looks good. Every craftsman knows this. His attitude to his work is 'to some degree aesthetic'. The nearer his craft is to fields of activity which have the function of giving delight, the stronger the aesthetic connexion will become. In sport and, especially, in dance, it is very strong indeed.

Training for social adequacy
The values here are the most workaday values in physical education. Though there is no reason whatever why they should not be fused with fun, with beauty and with pure motor satisfaction, their particular point is that they support the adequacy of the person in society —either society in general or the particular society in which he lives. Competence in the tasks of everyday life is something which is normally picked up in everyday living or acquired through the useful arts but there are many special skills and social refinements which may accrue from the activities of the physical education programme. Social forms of dance are an obvious example. Survival swimming is another. Many forms of athletic skill may, among other justifications, find value in enabling the individual to join in established community activities. One such activity is conversation. This may be thought somewhat removed from the world of physical education but one has only to think of cricket, with its rich background of skills and strategies, to say nothing of its literature, to

realise that to command it as a subject of civilised small talk, if no more, is a social asset.

A special group of 'athletic' skills of social and utilitarian value are those involved in lifting and carrying.

Training for fitness and health

Of all the values in physical education this is the oldest and best established. It comes nearest to being of self evident value. Whether we like it or not physical education (by whatever name it has been called) has in all ages derived support from the need for military fitness. To the Greeks gymnastics counterbalanced the softening influence of music by a concern for physical hardihood, physical resilience and physical health. The degree to which it is necessary or desirable to take the cultivation of physical power and stamina is a matter for discussion, leaving room for some difference of opinion and taste. The concept of fitness and the concept of health are both open to debate. But the person who will admit no interest in these matters is not likely to be interested in physical education.

Character Training

This is perhaps the most controversial of our value areas and the one where substantiation is the most difficult. The problems have been discussed in an earlier chapter and no more than a brief recapitulation will be attempted here.

There is considerable speculation about the effects on personality or character which may arise from an involvement in this or that form of vigorous physical activity such as games, dance or adventure pursuits. The difficulty is not in believing that effects on personality and character can take place. It is in predicting what these effects are likely to be. It may be thought that taking part in communal games and sports, particularly by young children, will encourage a certain physical hardihood and also an attitude of sociability. Many people believe this firmly. Fewer, perhaps, are concerned that the same tendencies, if carried to excess, may result in undue aggressiveness and insensitive behaviour. There is a long tradition of belief that outdoor pursuits react favourably upon personality and character, promoting especially self-reliance and sensitivity to natural beauty.

It would certainly be agreed that qualities such as self-reliance, sensitivity to beauty, physical courage and sportsmanship are qualities which develop slowly and precariously within the total education of the child. For any predictable effect the attitude and the quality of the teacher, parent or classmate is perhaps the over-riding consideration. But these agents need material through which to exert an influence. It seems reasonable to believe that the good physical education teacher will find such material within the scope of his activities.

Conclusion

The physical education teacher will not cultivate these values separately. He may not even be aware of them separately. He will see his field of activity as one in which physical sensation, fun, beauty and opportunities for training of various kinds fuse to promote an enrichment of living which encompasses education for the growing child. Enrichment of living is both the stuff and the end of education.

8: Curriculum

Curriculum is here interpreted as being an organisation of the content of varying 'subjects' or activities in the school life of the child. The structure of the curriculum can therefore be approached from two points of view: (*a*) the value (particularly the educational potential) of these varying 'subjects' or activities, and (*b*) the educational needs and administrative opportunities that arise at various points in the child's life and progress through the school.

In previous chapters physical education has largely been considered as a whole. Its areas of educational concern and its potential values have been investigated. On the assumption that it is still in the running as a credible unit in the total curriculum, the question of its own internal curricular organisation arises. One problem which has been encountered in considering physical education as a whole is that its activities fall into several distinct categories. It therefore seems necessary at this point to look at these categories in turn before attempting to comment upon the possible shape of the curriculum.

In a single chapter it is inevitable that attention should be focused on broad outlines rather than on points of detail. This may be thought to have some merit. Points of detail are often allowed to complicate general issues. In physical education it is probably true to say that it is upon the general issues rather than upon points of detail that there is the most urgent need for clarification. The following notes on the constituent elements and the chronological stages of the physical education curriculum are put forward as simply and as pointedly as possible, in an attempt to divest these matters of some of the mystique which surrounds them and to stimulate fundamental discussion.

CONSTITUENT ELEMENTS

Gymnastics

Of all the varied forms of gymnastics—turnen, sokol, remedial,

Swedish, primitive, Medau—only two are significant in English schools today. These are olympic gymnastics and educational gymnastics.

Olympic gymnastics is a form of acrobatics, deriving directly from the *turnen* of Jahn and now practised under national and international regulations as a sport. No form of gymnastics has ever been really popular in this country but there are signs that olympic gymnastics is beginning to take hold. It makes good television. It is a sport at which women's performance attracts as much attention as men's, or more. With the virtual disappearance of all other 'formal' gymnastics from the schools it now has a clear field.

Educational gymnastics is difficult to define or describe. It is 'informal'. Its aims are broad, rather than precisely defined and an observer might well get the impression that its scope is restricted rather by the physical limitations imposed by numbers and space than by any intrinsic limitations in the rationale of the activity. This broadness of scope is emphasised by the fairly common practice of referring to educational gymnastics simply as 'movement'.

In fact educational gymnastics concentrates on certain kinds of movement, to the exclusion of others. Members of the class are presented with a series of tasks—arranged around 'themes'—which they are free to perform in a manner more or less of their own devising. The tasks are essentially locomotor tasks demanding the exercise of a high degree of *agility* (where agility is seen as a compound of the qualities of strength, speed, mobility, balance and motor control). As in many other kinds of gymnastics, balance and control are often exercised in conditions of unusual body orientation. So, without being formally cultivated, the acrobatic element remains. The characteristic actions are those of climbing and swinging, jumping and vaulting, rolling and sliding, handwalking and somersaults. These actions are often simultaneously merged or combined in sequence. Throwing and catching—as in most other forms of gymnastics—are generally excluded. Lifting and carrying of a partner may appear in pair work. Evaluation is largely in terms of Laban's motion factors of time, space weight and flow.

There is no doubt that educational gymnastics can provide periods of vigorous, total body activity where large classes may take part under the control of one teacher. Interest in climbing, vaulting and the other skilled actions which figure in educational gymnastics may, for many people, be maintained, through adolescence, into adult life. Whether evaluation in Laban's terms will continue to hold attention is another matter. Some pupils will certainly be attracted away to other forms of activity such as rock climbing, diving, olympic gymnastics or dance where skills such as these can be more objectively appraised.

Dance

The modern orthodoxy is that since dance is an art form it must figure in schools as aesthetic education. This is not necessarily true. Subjects, whether they represent art forms or not, may be taught in schools for a variety of reasons.

Since the awareness of beauty is so fundamental as a cultural value, it will surely be fostered by sensitive teachers, whether of art, dance, woodwork or football. To this extent all education can be aesthetic education. In the more specific sense aesthetic education is education in the appreciation of the arts—the whole range of the arts. This is largely a contemplative function. Dance at some levels might contribute (and should never conflict) but surely dance in school and dance in society can be something else besides? It can be a satisfying human experience at many levels of significance. For the very young child it may bring a first recognition of pattern in movement—say through moving in a circle and all bobbing down together. For the older child, there is the recognition of subtler rhythms and the mastery of traditional forms, together with the opportunity for dramatic or comic display. For the adolescent, dance is pre-eminently the occasion on which boy meets girl. For the adult, in a community in which dance forms survive, dance is an opportunity for the expression of group membership and the acceptance of a tradition. For all participants dance provides the pleasures of untrammelled movement, skill and rhythm combined in an experience of peculiar emotive power.

The weakness of dance is its susceptibility to the effects of indiscipline and errors of taste. In the hands of a misguided tasteless teacher, or in the grip of tasteless fashion, dance can degenerate in a more spectacular way than any other art form. Being more 'personal', bad dance is more offensive than bad poetry or bad sculpture.

Educational dance today has made this vulnerability more apparent by rather turning its back on traditional forms. Even more than educational gymnastics it leaves one unsure, in advance, what the children are likely to be taught. Everything depends on the teacher. And critics may well fear that, being preoccupied with the idea of dance as a performing art, she may miss the opportunities presented by dance as an exhilarating physical experience and a social discipline.

It is the responsibility of leaders in the field to prove these fears wrong. The process may involve both the education of the critics and some change in the character of dance in schools.

Outdoor pursuits

This is a term used to cover a range of diverse activities from bird watching to climbing the Eiger. Motivation is of several distinct kinds, which may operate singly or combined. Firstly there is the love of country sights and sounds and an interest in nature. Secondly there is the enjoyment of physical activity and the exercise of certain locomotor skills. Thirdly there is the thrill of adventure.

The simplest activities are nature walks and cycle trips into the country. These are not primarily athletic occasions, though admission is generally made of the value of exercise and fresh air. Under the physical education banner the idea of exercise grows stronger, prompting more energetic and prolonged excursions, where enjoyment or study of the environment is something which must be combined with being vigorously on the move.

Camping is a natural corollary of field excursions. It involves an enjoyment of the simple life and it enables the participant to stay close to nature. Mobile camping, in particular, permits a domicile in remote places.

There are certain special locomotor skills, such as sailing, canoeing, rock climbing, riding and ski-ing, which can only be performed in an open country setting. These may all be performed for their own sake as sports, with no accompanying passion for outdoor pursuits as a way of life. But they very often arise from, or lead to, an interest in a particular outdoor environment and they may be cultivated as part of the more general ability required for certain forms of adventure activity.

The undertaking of adventurous excursions is for many, if not all, outdoor enthusiasts the culmination of their efforts. The degree of real danger may not be high. It is the function of skill and experience to keep this within reasonable bounds. But there will be challenge, novelty, uncertainty, suspense. Like competition in games these will add to the tension—and to the fun. And there will be the satisfaction of a real-life situation, demanding a competence to look after oneself and one's companions in conditions where survival may be at stake.

Quite young children may be introduced to the challenges and the joys of outdoor pursuits. They love climbing trees. Even some of the more complex skills such as ski-ing and riding, may, under favourable conditions, be acquired at an early age. Camping and midnight excursions have a particular fascination for young children. But as part of the physical education programme it is probable that organisational difficulties, the necessity for small parties, problems of transport and expense, to say nothing of the element of personal danger, will mean that outdoor pursuits figure mainly as an option, generally a popular one, for the older pupils.

Games and athletics

Games and athletics is a phrase which runs easily off the tongue of a physical educationist. Games and athletics has, for him, an identity, distinct from dance, distinct from outdoor pursuits, distinct from gymnastics. Yet the phrase covers a collection of rather different types of activity linked by the three ideas of play, competition and athletic movement.

Not all games are athletic. Bridge is distinctly unathletic. Billiards, though undoubtedly a game of high physical skill, is not athletic either. Even some of the physical play of young children does not involve total-body activity; such games as 'five stones' or 'knuckle bones' involve only hand movements and would not be thought to qualify, completely, for inclusion in the physical education curriculum.

Nevertheless when we think of the games of children and young people we usually think of the free moving, total-body activity, with a high skill content, which is the stuff of physical education. These are the games which we bracket with athletics.

The simplest are gamelike running activities often with the aid of some implement such as a skipping rope, hoop or whip and top. There are innumerable chasing games, like 'tag' and 'Mr. Wolf'. There are also aiming games like quoits and skittles. These last may involve the use of a ball but they are not true ball games; the ball is only a conveniently shaped missile.

Ball games are the great games. The ball (in badminton and ice-hockey it is not a ball) is never just a missile or a token. The game and the ball itself are so constructed that for much of the time the ball moves free of control and with a large degree of unpredictability. It seems to live.

It may serve as an interesting introduction to the 'anatomy' of ball games to classify them according to the part played by the ball. They appear to fall into four groups.

1. The ball is struck with the sole idea of controlling direction and distance. Such games are golf and croquet. These are never team games in the true sense, and the player and his opponent do not actively interfere in each other's play.

2. The ball is shuttled backwards and forwards. The object is to play your opponent's moving ball and force him into a position where he cannot play yours. Such games are tennis, badminton and volleyball over a net and squash, fives and pelota against a wall. In volleyball, a team element has been introduced into a type of game which is otherwise a singles, or, at most, a doubles game.

3. The ball is used to attack a defended position: it may be struck and runs scored while opponents recapture the ball before returning to the attack. Such games are cricket, rounders, baseball and long ball. They are essentially team games.

4. In all the preceding groups there is a clear understanding who is entitled to play the ball. Games in the fourth group are different. They involve a constant battle for possession of the ball. When captured the ball is carried or propelled towards a 'goal.' Such games are football, hockey, netball, basketball, lacrosse and polo. These are team games and games of incessant movement. Opponents are always in close proximity to one another. Bodily contact is either allowed or only avoided with difficulty. There is a premium on vigour and aggressive quality in the play.

'Athletics', as distinct from games, usually means what the Americans call 'Track and Field': competitive running, jumping and throwing. Swimming is not included with athletics but there is no logical reason for its separation. It is the same sort of activity but separate facilities happen to be necessary. Since feats of running, jumping, throwing and swimming can all be measured, either with tape or clock, it is possible to take part in satisfying objective practice without an active opponent. It is possible also to organise award schemes based on the achievement of standards. Even on a competitive occasion, jumping and throwing achievements are recorded and compared, rather than made in direct competition. The only athletic event in which competitors—and spectators—feel the full force of direct competition is a race.

Literature of various kinds has ascribed a prominent place to personal combat as a feature in the physical education of boys. The nineteenth century books on 'manly exercise' abound in references to the values of boxing, wrestling and fencing. (The one item of physical education in the prospectus of that redoubtable academy, Dotheboys Hall was 'single stick—if required'.) A Ministry of Education manual in 1936 devoted extensive sections to combat sports[1] and, writing in 1963, P. C. McIntosh rated them as one of the four divisions of the physical education curriculum which should be sampled by every boy.[2]

It would be interesting to know whether, at any time, there was widespread participation in these combat sports. Few boys ever seemed to take up competitive boxing, though one can remember that it was widely practised 'for fun' in the gymnasium. Now it is discredited because of the danger of head injury. Wrestling has never established itself in the schools and this is hardly to be regretted in view of the peculiarly unaesthetic forms which wrestling, professional and amateur, seems to take. Fencing remains a sport for the dedicated few. Among newer additions to the combat repertoire, Judo is an attractive and well-disciplined sport, suitable for both girls and boys. Karate, on the other hand, is by the most charitable estimate, morally dubious. To go through the motions of inflicting mortal injury on an opponent without the restraining reflection that one

---

[1] *Physical Recreation for Boys and Men.*
[2] P. C. McIntosh, *Practical Aspects of Physical Education*, P. E. A. Leaflet, Oct. 1963.

may receive an occasional blow oneself, seems more like thuggery than education.

One thing is certain: many boys, and some girls, who enjoy the element of inter-personal physical contest, find it not in a combat sport but in one of the ball games in category 4, above.

The competitive element in games and athletics accounts for their hold on public imagination and, because of this, leaves them open to exploitation by commercial, status-seeking or merely vulgar interests. These interests must be contested in the schools, but the fact that games and athletics are a matter of considerable concern in society at large is a sign of their vitality and should be held to increase, rather than diminish, their educational potential.

Few would deny that athletics and games, when taken together with the vast number of preparatory skill practices which occupy younger children and the fitness training programmes which appeal to more serious, older performers, provide the staple ingredient in what is known as physical education throughout the world.

CHRONOLOGICAL STAGES

There should be no rigid differentiation between the stages as set out below. Children develop at different rates and, in any case, each stage will merge with the next.

Infancy

In the very early years it is not meaningful to talk of physical education. All education is strongly physical in character. The child's total development is bound up with the acquisition of physical skills particularly those of manipulation, locomotion and speech.

Early School Years (5-9)

By the time the child arrives in school, the characteristic skills of the physical education or 'movement' programme—that is the skills of locomotion and control of moving objects—will have begun to differentiate themselves as forms of behaviour from the finer manipulatory skills and vocal skills which will have become organised as writing, art, handicraft and singing and from the more intellectual exercises of reading and number. It is no longer fashionable to regard these differing skills as distinct 'subjects' on a young child's timetable, but, as forms of civilised behaviour, they are distinguishable from one another and the child's advance in competence and maturity will demand the ability not only to see relationships between them but to concentrate attention and to make progress within the individual disciplines. In this context the skills involved in physical education, or movement or gymnastics (or call it what you will) begin to be seen as a discipline, not unrelated to others but having a set of concepts and methods of its own.

The movement programme in the early primary years will be designed to provide a liberal range of motor experience and opportunity for extensive skill acquisition. Acquisition of skill will constantly enrich the opportunities for experience and will also pave the way for advances in physical education at a later stage. The pace of advance should not be forced. Indeed it might be said that at this stage skills should not be actively *taught*. Opportunities, apparatus, space, encouragement should all be provided so that the child, of his own accord and at his own pace, will learn. But the distinction between active teaching and inspired direction of learning is always difficult to make. The skills at this stage are, or should be, such as will not demand the imparting of knowledge or techniques. The locomotor skills are those which will grow out of the child's discovery of his own bodily capacities, aided, of course, by his observation of the skilled movements of his fellows. The moving-object skills, in like manner, will grow out of the child's natural desire to capture and control such objects. The degree of success and failure will be clear. There are no rules to observe: no right and wrong way of doing things except those which bring the satisfaction of achieving the obvious objectives and enlarging the repertoire of skills. The teacher's function is to provide the opportunities, to maintain incentive and, through careful and skilled observation of the individual child, to steer him away from failure and towards success. This will demand sympathy, understanding and great skill on the part of the teacher. But it does not seem to demand the kind of skill commonly possessed by the physical education specialist. Some such specialists have been strikingly successful as advisers to teachers in infants schools but, under their guidance, many of the most successful teachers have been persons markedly lacking in either knowledge, training or competence at the more advanced athletic skills.

In the early years there does not seem to be any need to introduce, or any merit in introducing organised play. Experience shows that the young child will be completely absorbed by serious practice. He will be happy to work hard. His activity will be playlike in being free and spontaneous. There will be experiment and adventure: the element of fun will not be lacking, but there will be no 'let's pretend', no sets of rules and above all no competition. It will not be a game: it will be the real thing.

Of special importance at this stage will be the provision for those locomotor practices which will not normally be found outside school. Prominent among these will be climbing and swimming. Climbing apparatus of many kinds is now commonplace in infants and junior schools. It is not so common to find opportunities for the learning of swimming. Yet where such opportunities exist, or where enlightened parents themselves take young children to the pool, results are strikingly good in terms of enjoyment, confidence and, eventually, learning to swim.

A point that may influence teaching method, if not curriculum content, is that teachers of infants' classes seem to agree in maintaining that the movement lessons are of especial value as a vehicle for social training. One headmistress of a Leeds infants school, noted for its excellent movement programme, puts as the last of her four objectives: 'To develop an awareness of other children in their movement, particularly in the sharing of space and apparatus'.[1] This opinion may serve as encouragement for those teachers who believe that more sophisticated experience in practical morality is not impossible higher up the school.

Dance, even with very young children does seem to demand special aptitude and special training on the part of the teacher. Whereas for other locomotor forms, even for swimming, children can at this stage be provided with the opportunities and, with a minimum of guidance, be allowed to learn, dance needs to be skilfully taught.

In the later primary years skill practices will increase in complexity. The locomotor practices will become organised as educa-

---

[1] H. Stuttard, personal communication, 1968.

tional gymnastics and the moving object practices, particularly ball skills, will begin to assume a more sophisticated character and eventually will find expression in simple pair activities and small group games.

A final note. In case it should be thought that the virtual exclusion of formal teaching will unduly restrict the physical activities practised by children of this age it is suggested that the following list of locomotor and moving object skills are skills which the child, given the encouragement and the opportunity, may 'learn for himself': running, skipping, chasing, dodging, balancing, climbing (ladders, ropes, trees), swinging, leaping, vaulting, swimming, throwing for distance, aiming, catching and trapping with hand and foot, kicking, striking with hand, stick or racquet, juggling, hand walking, somersaults and simple acrobatics of many kinds.

With suitable opportunities the child of this age may also have learned to ride a bicycle or a pony, to roller skate or to ski.

The middle school years (9-13)

It should go without saying that anything which is true about the physical education needs of children of this age is true whether or not they are accommodated in an institution designated as a 'middle school'. None the less it is of value to look at these needs in particular relationship to the middle school at this moment, because, in the general lack of consensus among politicians, administrators and teachers about the form and function of this new institution, no group has been more conspicuously inarticulate than physical educationists. The matter is of prime importance because the quality and the nature of physical education depends so much upon the facilities provided and if boys and girls are to be housed in particular schools during these middle years it is essential that the facilities should be right for their needs. They cannot share the facilities of children younger or older than themselves.

In default of a middle school policy—at any rate among physical educationists—it seems that the ethos and methods of the primary school are likely to spread upwards into the middle school. The following notes are written in the firm belief that the normal boy or girl of nine years of age ought to be moving on from primary school physical education (that is physical education dominated by ideas of experiment and discovery and only minimally concerned with technique). Equally the boy or girl of nine to thirteen is not ready for secondary school physical education which is geared to the needs of a fairly mature, autonomous individual, approaching adult life.

The middle years are an opportunity to introduce the child to a comprehensive range of established physical activities. He should, by now, be 'a good mover'; agile in his locomotion and competent in the control of balls and other moving objects. He has ample physical energy and is not oppressed by academic demands. He is still willing to follow, without question, any reasonably interesting programme laid down by the teacher. Experiment and discovery will, of course, continue, but they should no longer dominate the learning process. The need is for the child to learn techniques and to comprehend forms of organisation which he could never discover for himself and he must learn them quickly. Nevertheless the aim is not primarily a high level of excellence. This can come later. If technical excellence is allowed to assume too great an importance at this stage it will impede the teacher's ability, (a) to hold the interest of the less able performers and (b) to cover a wide programme. The aim at this stage should be initiation. The form of the initiation, the identification of essentials, the order in which things are presented as well as the actual technique of the presentation—all this will demand expert teaching of a very high quality. What is needed is a teacher who may not be a 'county standard' performer but who has been thoroughly trained in the techniques, the rules, the tactics and the traditions of a comprehensive repertory and trained also in the art of teaching. Is not this the physical education 'specialist'?

Difficulties immediately present themselves to the imagination. Physical education specialists are in short supply. How are they to be attracted and how integrated into the middle schools? And how are the facilities to be devised and provided? If such a scheme were to operate it might well mean that middle schools would be equipped with sports halls, covered areas and all-weather pitches suitable for an intensive programme and staffed with physical educationists even at the expense of the high schools. There would be room for some imaginative planning. Pitches could be smaller, equipment could be modified and organisation simplified to enable these younger children to learn the essentials fast.

Without these opportunities children in the middle years will probably continue to spend the bulk of their physical education periods doing educational gymnastics. This is economical of space, time and equipment and it demands no great versatility on the part of the teacher. If well taught it is vigorous, varied and enjoyable activity. But nowadays even enthusiasts are heard to express the belief that educational gymnastics has served its purpose, for most children, by the time they reach their early teens. It might well be phased out earlier than this.

The later school years (after 13)

A matter of major concern in physical education during these years will be the approaching transfer to after-school, adult life. Not the least of the difficulties attending this transfer is that, after he has left school, the young person will find that the activities he has known in the physical education programme will be regarded by most of his fellow adults as, perhaps, commendable but not in any way essential. Physical education will have become physical recreation. Even if he goes to college or university, where extensive facilities are provided, he will be quite free to ignore them altogether if he wishes. The physical education teacher need sacrifice none of his own belief in the value of his commodity when he accepts this state of affairs. After all physical recreation, as non-obligatory, is in the very good company of music, art, poetry and the theatre, to say nothing of philosophy and religion. It seems reasonable to believe that the physical education programme during the later years at school should be a preparation for this change and that such a preparation can be best effected by a progression from the required programme of earlier years, through a programme of options to a final programme—say for the last year at school—which is purely voluntary. During this final voluntary period provision would be made and encouragement would be given but, as a deliberate training device, the decision whether or not to take part would be left to the pupil himself.

The adoption of such a policy would, of course, present an additional challenge to the physical education staff. It would entail a determined and continuing effort on their part to keep in touch with the tastes and interests of individual boys and girls. Anything approaching complete success would hardly be attainable. But the degree of continuing participation might be a useful criterion of success to add to those more commonly in use, such as the performance of the school teams.

Whether or not requirement is retained it would seem realistic with senior pupils to provide for participation at two levels of involvement. For those with talent and inclination there should be provision for high level performance. For others standards of performance can, and in many cases should be forgotten, except those minimally necessary for the achievement of fun.

Provision for participation at these two levels would necessitate some functional divisions in the programme. The serious performers at a particular activity must practise together. But there need be no complete separation of sheep from goats among the pupils. A boy may be interested in swimming at high level competition and in table tennis just for fun. Furthermore having taken up table tennis just for fun he may become interested in performance standards and begin to put in serious practice. The point is that at this stage, and in adult life beyond, recreation is considered by most people to be a perfectly adequate justification. This may be deplored by some physical educationists who see it as downgrading their subject to the level of a compensatory function, compared with the largely developmental function of earlier years. But compensation for the stresses of adolescent and adult life is no unworthy function. Physical recreation, as purely compensatory activity, can be closely linked with a concern for total health.

The idea that senior boys and girls should be largely free to choose their physical activities might involve some modifications in the accepted provision of facilities. The changes might not be so great as expected. Team games need not disappear. Quite the reverse. But for the less dedicated pupils the organisation might be simplified and the competitive pressures reduced. Forms of soccer, rugby, hockey and cricket can be devised where, without contributing much in the way of skill, without giving up too much time and without fear of ridicule, the less able pupils may get maximum action and maximum fun. Experience in universities, where for some time physical education departments have run voluntary programmes, indicates that, where there is a large population of young people, team games played at the 'fun' level are among the most popular activities. To simplify the organisation and satisfy the demand, experiments are being made with shorter games, smaller teams and smaller, often non-grass pitches. These developments may prove to be more than expedients. They may prove to have positive merit. For the less gifted and the less active player (as for the younger child in the middle school) there is a certain merit in a small pitch.

Nevertheless a comprehensive recreative programme must provide for more than team games. There should be the opportunity for the individual to go for a swim, to train on his own in the gymnasium or jog round the field. There should be classes in ballroom and social dancing where boys and girls are partners. And there should be provision for activities in pairs, of which the most popular are the racquet games.

The other level of participation—the serious pursuit of high standards—necessitates the introduction of certain elements which have not previously appeared in the physical education programme. These are (a) high level specialist coaching in particular aspects of games, athletics, gymnastics and dance, (b) fitness training programmes, and (c) the formation of school clubs to foster interest and to promote competitions.

Physical education at the high school as at the primary and middle schools will largely be effected through physical participation but at the more senior level it seems appropriate to introduce some study of human physical activity from a purely intellectual point of view. Firstly there might be teaching about the relationship between activity, fitness and health. This could link up with the fitness training programmes provided for the more athletically motivated pupils. Secondly, opportunities might be taken to interest pupils in scientific, sociological or aesthetic studies related to aspects of skilled movement, sport or dance. The gym might, at times, become an exercise laboratory and the dance studio might provide a window onto social history and the arts. Linked with a study of movement mechanics, there might well be a course of training in the work skills of lifting, pulling, pushing and carrying. These more intellectual and utilitarian exercises need not detract from the appeal of the activity. In fact they might enhance it, since they are in tune with the more adult attitude which can be expected of pupils at this age.

It will be seen that the teacher responsible for physical education in the high school has differing functions from his counterpart in the middle school. His opportunities for experiment and response to suggestion are wider. His duties are much less easily defined. He may not be competent to teach some of the activities in his programme but he must be competent to decide on the suitability of those who do. The conditions under which professional coaches, who are not teachers, may play a part in the programme is a matter which will demand his particular attention. The physical educationist at this stage must have the qualities not only of a good teacher but of a good administrator. He must be able to devise an imaginative programme and to inspire the pupils and the other teachers who are working with him with his own concern for the inter-relationship of health and activity, culture and skill.

Subject Index